# Pretty Things
# For
# Nice People

## Tales of Patrons & Artisans

The Challenges and Triumphs of
20th Century Artisans In New York

Joseph Fiebiger

For information, address Enlightening Publishers, LLC
105 Eototo Road, El Prado, NM 87529
Email: publishers@icloud.com

First Edition
1 2 3 4 5 6 7 8 9 0
Printed in the United States of America
Library of Congress Cataloging-in-Publication Data
Joseph Fiebiger, 1944
Pretty Things For Nice People — 1st ed.
Summary: History of P.A. Fiebiger, Inc., a New York City based company of metal artisans.
The patrons, and stories that drove the commissions. Indepth attention to the
Restorations of The Statue of Liberty and Ellis Island in the 1980's.
ISBN 13: 978-0692303627
ISBN 10: 0692303626

[1. Identity-Non-Fiction. 2. Artistic Metal Work 3. Statue of Liberty Restoration. 4. United States Capitol.
5. Central Park, New York City] I. Title.

Front Cover Art: ©Gary #5278299, Fotolia

Back Cover Art: ©John Anderson #10518673, Fotolia

Visit www.enlighteningpublishers.com

# *Sincere Thanks*

Naturally thanks to my life partner and wife, Balinda. She listened to all of this stuff, ad nauseam, until it had a personality of its own (we hope).

Deepest thanks to the late Charles Ryskamp who placed the bee in bonnet to write this work. He said, "I'll edit for you. I'm serious, Joe. The stories are part of the art."

Many thanks to Martha Hackley, of The Frick Collection; Theodore S. Bartwink, of the Harkness Foundation For Dance; Stephen T. Ayers, Architect of the Capitol; Barbara Wolanin, Curator of the Capitol, Amy Elizabeth Burton, Office of the Senate Curator; Theodore Ceraldi, Timothy Lynch, Michael Lynch, Richard Hanington, Arthur Coyner, James Semans, and Mary Biddle Duke Semans.

Gratitude indeed to the Statue of Liberty's great historical archivist at the Bob Hope Memorial Library at Ellis Island, Barry Moreno.

More thanks: The preferred photographer of the Statue of Liberty / Ellis Island Foundations Peter B. Kaplan for his photographs and factual editing for Lady Liberty; Stephen Briganti of the Statue of Liberty / Ellis Island Foundation.

Paul August Fiebiger　　　　　　　　Paul James Fiebiger

Back Row: Walter Gonzalez, Florencio Perez
Middle Row: Joe Karhut, Joseph Fiebiger, Antonion Del Vecchio
Front Row: Gennaro (Bruno) Ranieri

Dedicated to

Opa, Dad,

Gennaro "Bruno" Ranieri

and

all of the multi-talented men who made these works.

And to the patrons who gave us the privilege to serve the art that we all loved.

Thanks to the foreman / artisan  for Paul August Fiebiger,

remembered today by the author as Joseph.

Thanks to the talented Alfonso De Pippo who worked

with Paul James Fiebiger.

And thanks to Florencio "Amigo" Perez,

Joseph Karhut

and Master Craftsmen  / Artisan,

Gennaro "Bruno" Ranieri.

# *Publisher's Note*

In order to keep publishing costs to a minimum, this book is published with black and white photographs.

The color versions of the photographs can be viewed at:

http://enlighteningpublishers.com

or

http://www.pafiebiger.com

# Table of Contents

# Chapter 1
## Opa

"Sex hour? Hell! We didn't even have a coffee break!" That was my grandfather's response when asked about his first job in America. Always "Opa" to me, he had emigrated from Germany in 1898. His first job was as a foreman/blacksmith for The Sexaur Iron Works in New York City.

He chose to hitch his wagon to his own star and began P.A. Fiebiger Ironworks in New York City in May 1900. Dad, born four years later, became his partner as soon as he was old enough.

Opa worked on the forge until his 88th year. He said the reason he lived so long was that he saw what water did to iron, so he only drank wine. No kidding! He even brushed his teeth with wine.

Opa made a specially designed hand truck to transport damaged electric

406 Tenth Avenue
(Between 33rd & 34th Streets)
New York, NY
Circa 1917

*The young man on the right is Paul James Fiebiger*

motors to the motor re-winding company on Tenth Avenue at 38th Street and also to transport two, five-gallon jugs of wine from the liquor store at Tenth Avenue 42nd Street. The truck was designed for a young boy to be able to pull it and navigate the curbs without damaging either the motors or the wine.

The New York City Police Department converted Ninth and Tenth Avenues from two-way to one-way in 1948. Ninth Avenue was southbound, Tenth Avenue northbound. Eleventh Avenue remained two-way. There were no curb cuts to provide handicap access or allow a young boy easy navigation. Our shop was located on the Southeast corner of 36th Street and Tenth Avenue, at the mouth of the Lincoln Tunnel in the heart of Hell's Kitchen.

Legend has it that Hell's Kitchen got its name from the most prominent Irish gin mill in the area, "Halley's Bar." Ironically, its supposed underworld prom-

*Southeast Corner of Tenth Avenue and 36th Street*
*Before construction of the Lincoln Tunnel*
*Ca. 1932*

inence made it safe. Each of these businesses paid a dollar a week to "Merchants Protection Agency." Who they were? No one ever knew. Safety was guaranteed to those who kept proverbial "clean noses."

The avenues and side streets were always busy with cars, trucks, buses and cabs. Always moving, always stopping, always noisy. The sidewalks were lined with light manufacturing buildings like ours, and tenement houses. Usually five-story walk-ups with businesses on the ground floors. Butchers, grocers, bakers, restaurants, bars, cobblers, tailors, dry cleaners, motor re-winders, liquor stores, auto parking lots and auto repair facilities dotted the neighborhood.

As I walked along the avenue, and crossed it, I smelled the smells of the city, heard its sounds, and knew its heartbeat. I was never frightened.

*462 Tenth Avenue Shop*
*Man in the center is a more mature Paul James Fiebiger*
*Ca. 1923*

My father, years later, reflected that the area was safer with the "protection" than with the police.

The main floor of the shop was 25 feet wide by 60 feet long. The forge area was outside the rear of the building, enclosed with a structural steel angle iron network that supported the corrugated metal roof. The area was the width of the building and 15 feet long. There was one power hammer and two coal fired forges. They were covered with an iron hood that vented up five stories to pass the roof line. The fireboxes of the forges were driven by electric motors with air gates to adjust the flow of air and control the heat of the fire.

There were also two forges and two power hammers one floor below, in the basement. During the 1920s those forges were used, as my father said, "by very talented and temperamental smiths. They wouldn't forge scrolls or hammer leaves, only figures for hardware or andirons. I only saw them to give them sketches, pay envelopes or hear their requests for more iron or more coal." He always had a wry smile when he talked about them and their peculiar and beautiful world.

The main forge was dimly lit so that the blacksmiths could easily determine the color of the iron as it was heated. Though the firebox was dim, the surrounding work area was lighted appropriately. White hot, curiously named "snowball heat," is approximately 2,200 degrees Fahrenheit. Dull red, the opposite end of the heat spectrum, is 1,600 degrees Fahrenheit. The hotter the iron, the easier it is to forge to the desired shape. The art of the smith is the synthesis of heat, power and speed.

I learned to remove the spent dull black little chunks of burned coal, called "clinkers" from the coal fireboxes as a six year old. I stood on a milk crate to use the drill press at eight. Learning then had no age boundaries, I watched as the band saw cut material, made polishing wheels with glue and emery powder,

4

painted with red lead, melted lead and used hand files. The process was never ending, as I grew bigger I performed harder physical tasks, but I also was taught estimating, designing, laying out and finally the rudiments of the forge, repoussé and the taking of templates.

Curved stair railings required precise templates. They were the hardest jobs we ever had and we had plenty of them. Templates are taken by hammering an iron bar to the gentle curve that defines the shape of the stair while marking the risers and treads. A 1/16 of an inch error at the bottom would be amplified to one inch at the top. The work is heavy yet delicate.

I was fascinated by the physics of the machinery and how we made things. The logic mixing with the art was compelling. Poor Dad, I drove him crazy with my constant barrage of questions. He had me keep a small notebook and write down questions to be answered while driving or at dinner. A routine that we grew to savor.

I had learned how to use the "Steel Manual" to determine the weights of various sizes of materials. Simple arithmetic extended the weights to a dollar amount. I said, "Dad, since you don't charge for iron, why do you bother to figure it?"

"Good question. We don't charge for iron because it's the way the old world artisans showed respect to their patrons. But we use that information, we know that cost of the iron is about one percent of the job. We just use it to cross check the labor estimates."

I learned at an early age that one of the beautiful facets of this business was that you could never, ever know enough and that you learned something new every day. I believed the aphorism, "If you stand still you go backwards."

My parents were my best friends. I wondered when I went off to college in 1961. They had hoped that I would study French and attend the École des Beaux Arts and become an architect. As I departed I took a snapshot through the car window. Mom, with her "garbage blonde hair" that we all teased her about, her nice figure, pretty face and gravelly voice, She stood with her arm around Dad's waist. His brown eyes ran like deep pools, her blue ones like a calm sky. Everything about them said that they loved me deeply.

I returned home from college in the summer of 1963 to find out that the business was on hard times. Dad was worried that people's desire for fine metal work had waned. He said, "Maybe mediocre is okay now? I don't know. Maybe we just need some young thinking,"

"Mine?" I asked.

"Naturally. You probably know more than you think. Maybe you'll even grow to like the business. I'll try to make it easier for you. Just keep an eye of everything."

That summer I watched the men work on the forge. I studied their movements and how those movements related to the heat in the iron. I stayed late, worked on my own. I got frustrated many times. If a piece that I made was subpar I destroyed it. I didn't want the men to see them. Dad saw the pieces and understood why I burned them.

"You know, Joe, it'll come to you. You don't have know everything perfectly, just knowing how to do it is enough. The men will always be better than you are. Just don't let your inability to make something prevent you from designing it."

We had moved from Manhattan to New Rochelle, N.Y., in 1952. Quite proudly, I was the first "kid" to come through the New Rochelle Little League as a player and return to coach. I played semi-pro baseball for the New Rochelle

Robins. In 1965 everything changed. Dad needed a major surgical procedure. I had to take over.

The operation required that we replenish in a ratio of two to one, the blood used during the operations. We owed a lot of blood; no money, just blood. Every player on the Robins knew and liked Dad. Everybody liked Dad! Each of them gave a pint of blood to satisfy our debt to the blood bank. Forty-three years later, at an Old Timer's Day game, when I thanked them again, they all remembered.

I went to the shop and told the men our family situation. Three of them said that they wanted to take their vacations – starting now. One mumbled something and quit. One stayed and we carried on.

With all of God's good graces, we survived and eventually thrived. This was certainly not the first, nor would be it be last time, that I asked God, "Please let me be better than I am. Just for a little while."

# Chapter 2
# Father Spellman

Architects Lewis Adams and Frederick Woodbridge extended their friendship to my father when they expanded my learning curve. Guenter, the only remaining employee and I worked to finish the ongoing job at Trinity Church, Wall Street. Once completed , there were no jobs in the queue.

Once again a prayer was answered. On a warm and sunny September day in 1965, a priest came through the front door of the shop with sun shining on his shoulders and through his white hair. He looked like an angel. He said, "I was told that if I walked along Tenth Avenue I would find someone to make the railings and gates that I need for my Church. Was I told right, son?"

I introduced myself to him, shook his hand and met his warm blue eyes with my brown ones, "Father, would you like a glass of schnapps?"

He smiled and said, "I would like that."

"Come with me, please," I climbed the spiral stairway to the office and explained that this stash was from my father's collection and offered him a variety of spirits. He choose the scotch. As we sat, he asked me how I was and what was happening in my life. My words and my tears poured out. I explained how my father was fighting for his life, how I was still taking university courses while running the business and how frightened I was.

His eyes were soft as they played over me. When he spoke his voice was a soft melody, a fibre of caring running through it. He extended one hand toward me and said, "Son, can you make these railings and gates for me?"

I couldn't speak, so I nodded. He asked that I meet him at his Queen of Angels Roman Catholic Church in Long Island City the next day. I accompanied him down the spiral stair to the front doors. As he left he said,

"I will pray for you and your family. God Bless."

As he exited the building, the setting sun cast a glow of white all around him. I watched him as walked up Tenth Avenue. Guenter, silent witness to these events was smiling.

I went home and told my father about the events of the day. He was still bedridden and in a great deal of pain, but he understood everything and smiled.

I met Father Spellman the next day and brought our design folders for the categories of gates and railings. He chose relatively simple motifs and asked that I prepare an estimate for him as quickly as possible. There were many stair railings and a set of driveway gates.

I met him the next evening at the Warwick Hotel lounge and gave him a written proposal. He looked at it and said, "I would have given this job to you no matter what." I drove him back to his Rectory in Long Island City. He asked me to wait downstairs and went to his apartment and came back down with a gift for me. We sat down and he explained the Prayer of St. Joseph that he had given to me, came with his special blessing. I have always carried that prayer with me.

Guenter and I breezed through the stair railings. Straight railings are always simple. I was gaining confidence. But then came the gates. Strong, yet delicate, easy pivoting, designed to make climbing hard but not impossible. Still, they had to be square, level and plumb. But did they really have to be square?

I had been thrown into the fire! Dad had always said that we make gates differently than any one else. We purposely build them out of square to allow for them to sag, and though they would not be square, they would be level and plumb. I asked my father what our special ratio was. Still confined to his bed, still in pain, he said "one sixteenth of an inch to the foot."

We made the gates out of square. Guenter and I dug the holes for the

Hand forged angel of peace
Ca. 1290

pivoting mechanisms. We poured the concrete, let it set and then we put the gates in place. They were too high in the center! The brass Cross was sitting askew. The gates didn't sag, they ran uphill. The ratio was too unforgiving. What to do? We removed the gates and took them back to the shop. But what ratio was right? I gently asked Dad what to do. Almost as if he didn't remember my asking the first time, he said, "Set it one thirty-second of an inch to the foot up from square."

We made this correction and sure enough the gates worked perfectly. Level, plumb, pivoting easily and hard to climb. The cross sitting proudly plumb.

As this job neared its completion, Dad was beginning to feel better. He wanted to meet Father Spellman; Father Spellman sure wanted to meet him. In early December Dad and I went to Queen of Angels.

Father Spellman and my Dad were two kindred souls. The warmth between them was deep. Father Spellman praised me and my father beamed. Father Spellman explained how he and his congregation had prayed for my father and for our family. We all cried.

Dad said, "Father Spellman, I am going to ask Joe to make something special for you and it will be my gift to you and your church. It's an Angel of Peace from the Catholic Church in Wittichenau, Germany. The original Angel of Peace is Gabriel sounding his horn, welcoming Crusading soldiers home. It was forged of iron, around 1290. My father, returned to his home in Germany after World War I to find that the church bells had been smelted for war matériel. He gave the church money to replace the bells and in gratitude, the church fathers gave to him, this Angel of Peace.

We recently completed a very extensive commission for Paul Mellon in Upperville, Virginia. Mellon built Trinity Episcopal Church as a gift. We had the privilege of doing all of the ironwork for fifteen years. In keeping with the tradition of the artisan and patron, we offered this original Angel of Peace as a gift to the Church. Architect, Page Cross designed a lighting fixture for the entrance, incorporating the original Angel and two bronze replications."

We had a few extra Angels cast at the time.

I quickly fitted the Angel to have a proper mount and Guenter and I installed it. Then Father Spellman asked that Dad, Mom and I return for the Dedication of the Angel of Peace at Queen of Angels Roman Catholic Church.

# *Chapter 3*
## *Trinity Episcopal Church*
## *Upperville, Virginia*

Page Cross designed this Norman French church for his Yale University roommate, Paul Mellon. Mellon and his wife, Bunny, had a country house and stable, Rokeby Farm in nearby Middleburg, Virginia.

Cross' signature talent was his attention to minutiae. Drawings were prepared for each piece of fieldstone and each piece of decorative wood work. Cross' talented designer, Arthur Taylor, designed the stair railings, grilles, chandeliers, lecterns, hinges, locks, signs, and hardware. Dad used to kid that Taylor even designed every hammer blow.

Dad said that this commission was a labor of love for all the craftsmen. He said that he had never had such an experience before. He explained that even during the Depression we survived because of the patrons' love of the artisans. I later asked Cross if he agreed. He said that it was that way for him and his staff. This was a once in lifetime commission.

Eighty-eight years old, five foot–eight inches tall weighing 140 pounds soaking wet, a full head of grey hair, Opa forged all of the nails and helped with the hinges. The other smiths did the heavier work. But Opa loved those nails. When all was said and done we had barrels of them.

I grew up on this commission and made many trips to Virginia. Dad said that if he "kept me in his pocket," that I would learn. So this was osmosis?

I grew up in suburban, liberal, New Rochelle and had not been aware of racial discrimination. I was on athletic teams with what were then called "colored" players and had friends that were "colored." Richard Roundtree, the actor, actually may have saved my life in a schoolyard scuffle. Yet it was in Virginia that I witnessed racial discrimination. So abhorrent to me! Nonetheless it was mandated that I keep my mouth shut and go about my business.

As the commission in Upperville neared completion my father offered the Angel of Peace, with its history, as his and his Opa's gift to the new Trinity Church.

The Mellons accepted graciously, and Cross designed the lighting fixture

*Hand forged chandeliers*

that incorporated the Angel.

The motif called for three of the angels, the original and two cast bronze replicas. Again, some years later, while driving with Cross, he explained that this gift had engendered the spirit that the Mellon's had hoped for when they donated the Church.

*Hand carved wood pulpit with hand forged iron lectern*

# Chapter 4
## Frank Stanton

It was not unusual for a stretch limo to be parked at the Tenth Avenue curb in front of the shop. A long black one pulled up on an August morning in 1968. A well dressed gentlemen and his chauffeur entered.

Florencio, whom we nicknamed, Amigo, called upstairs to the office in his native Spanish. Amigo always struggled with slang and figures of speech. He fumbled them, but he always got his messages across with smiles.

Amigo was a Cuban refugee. He and our visitors were engaged in conversation, in Spanish, when I walked down the spiral stair. My Spanish was passable and I understood the visitor to say that he had traveled to Cuba many times in better days and had always loved it.

Frank Stanton introduced himself and his chauffeur while he gave me his business card. All it had printed on it was, "Frank Stanton, CBS, New York City" and the CBS logo.

Stanton asked if we could repair an antique, delicate cast iron trivet that his wife had loved. She had just passed away and he expressed his sadness. The chauffeur pulled an object from a small shopping bag. Stanton said that they had been to other iron works and were told that such mending was either impossible or very difficult and might destroy the piece.

Amigo and I looked at it and smiled. Repairing this was truly a simple matter.

A doubtful expression had come to Stanton's face. "How," he asked, "are you going to do this?"

I explained that special welding rods with high nickel content were required. I explained that the real "trick" was to bury the piece in the hot coals of the forge. Both the coals and the piece would cool down together.

That won his trust. I told him that it would be completed by day's end.

The process was very simple and didn't take much time. The time was spent in the cooling.

The chauffeur arrived the next morning to pick it up. He asked me to either give him an invoice or send it to Stanton. I said that there was no charge. He took the now cooled, cast iron artifact and left with a smile.

Early the next morning the limo reappeared. The chauffeur carried packages as he entered the building. He explained that Stanton was very touched and grateful. He expressed his gratitude with hundreds of Columbia Records--LP albums. He said, "The boss picked the Spanish/Cuban albums personally. He wanted to be sure that there were a lot of *Quisas, Quisas, Quisas* and *Quando Salí de Cuba*."

Amgio, sensing my bewilderment, shrugged sheepishly and said, "He asked me what my favorite songs were. I told him."

I called the switchboard for CBS and asked to speak with Stanton. His secretary asked me to identify myself and in a moment he came on the line. He thanked me and wanted to make sure that Amigo liked his music. I told him that he was very appreciative.

He said that he would come get me for coffee some morning and that we would go to everybody's favorite, the Empire Diner on 22nd Street and Tenth Avenue. A nice thought, but it never happened.

# *Chapter 5*
# *John D. Rockefeller, Sr.*

Opa was a favored artisan of the architects William Delano and his partner Chester Aldrich. John D. Rockefeller, Sr. had commissioned them in 1906 to design *Kykuit* (rhymes with "high cut), for his estate in Westchester. The architecturally spectacular, Greek-Roman style house was completed in 1913

Central Park's landscape architect Frederick Law Olmsted was chosen to landscape grounds. He fell from grace and was discharged after he told Rockefeller, "the grounds will be mature in twenty years," He sited Central Park as an example. Senior designed the grounds himself and

Kykuit
Pocantico Hills, New York
Delano and Aldrich, Architects

planted mature trees.

Some of the original ironwork on the estate was purchased in Europe. The works were drawn to scale by an architect of the firm, disassembled by local craftsmen, numbered and shipped to America. Opa installed them.

Exterior gates and fences were easy. There were no precise dimensions that had to be maintained. They did not attempt curved stair railings. How could you accurately build the stair to the railing? Easier to make the railing anew, just make prototypes and reproduce them here. According to Opa's tales, the window grilles and balcony railings were also simple. They hit a noteworthy snag when the size of a window grille was right, but the number of windows was wrong. They had two grilles and three windows.

How to make two additional window grilles without damaging the original? Impossible! Opa took the original apart and made three new. He put the original back together and it was put in storage on the estate.

In the mid 1950's much of the exterior ironwork was in need of restoration. Noted architect, Mott B. Schmidt, in his mid fifties was commissioned. Opa and Dad worked in concert with Schmidt for the restoration.

The primary reason the restoration was required after approximately fifty years was attributed to red lead paint that had been used. Now deemed a carcinogen, it had a life of forty to fifty years.

Driveway gates, pedestrian gates, window grilles, stair railings and balcony railings encompassed the twelve years of restoration. My contribution, as an athletic boy of twelve, was to scale gates and get to the over-gate panel to release the crane's hook. They had padded my foot falls and hand holds and I scampered twenty feet into the air and released the hook. When got down, I asked my father, "Can I have my banana now?'

In 1977 we were called to the estate to make some relatively minor repairs to entrance gates and to restore the bronze doors of the Tea House.

This should have been a straightforward commission.

Nelson A. Rockefeller was Vice-President of the United States. Naturally, he was under the protection of the Secret Service. When we first attempted to perform the remedial work on the entrance gates, helicopters descended from the sky and agents disembarked. Guns drawn. What had we done? Easily explained, one would think, yet it took three more false alarms until the Secret Service decided to keep an agent with us.

The glass and verdigris bronze Tea House was set well within the perimeter. Security was not an issue. When we disassembled the door frames we found that newspaper had been used as caulking.

As I unfolded the "caulking" I found articles from the sports section of the 1914 issue of *Boston Globe*. There was a baseball story and the box score from a game in which Babe Ruth had pitched and batted for Red Sox.

I asked a preservationist at the Morgan Library to save it. She tried, but it had been folded too tightly.

When we reinstalled the doors, instead of newspaper we used silicone caulking. Babe Ruth doesn't live in the Tea House anymore.

# *Chapter 6*
## *The Library of Presidential Papers, New York*

We were awarded the commission to make fences and gates with a Greek Key frieze motif for front of The Library of Presidential Papers. The Library was founded by Henry O. Dormann in 1966 and was located at 17 East 80th Street. A polished bronze moulding sat atop the ironwork to produce a blend of pleasing colors. The most notable element of the design was the bronze *Seal of the President of The United States* mounted on each gate. These plaques were cast as *bas reliefs* with a statuary (chocolate) background and polished foreground.

Opa made two cast bronze door stops of the *Seal of the President of The United States* for the Harding administration. We had the repoussé pattern and its full size drawing. Architectural drawings and the full size drawing were submitted to the White House for approval.

Secret Service agents visited while we worked. They had reviewed the drawings and noted that the polished bronze handrail mouldings were fastened with flat head brass screws. Good craftsmanship mandated that the screws not pierce the top surface, hence the name "blind fastening."

Agents requested that the handrails either be dropped from the design or brazed. An agent said to me, "We don't want them coming off, the hell with craftsmanship."

No argument from me, we used the screws and set them too deeply in the support member. Then we brazed and ground them to be invisible.

We always had a Christmas party for the men, gifts for them, their wives, and their children. It was great fun. A week later we repeated the party. Again we ordered a famous six-foot-long sandwich from Manganaros, had some spirits and welcomed in the New Year. We had been doing this forever.

On December 31, 1970 with our New Year's Eve party in full force, a phone call came through.

"Joe Fiebiger?"

"This is he."

"Are you a Nixon warmonger?'

"Who is this?" I asked.

"Well are you?"

"No!"

"This is Paul Newman. I am at The Library of Presidential Papers and I want to know why you turned the Eagles heads to face the arrows?"

When his voice dropped somewhat I managed to squeeze in, "Can you explain this to me?"

He had visited with Doorman at the Library. Doorman told him to call me for an explanation.

I never doubted that it was the famous actor. He was one of my favorites. I thought I recognized his voice. But here, now, he was most certainly not Fast Eddie Felson in *The Huster*. More like an angry, *Hud*.

Explain he did. Before 1945 *The Seal of the President of The United States* had the Eagles heads facing the thirteen arrows. Obviously

*Presidential Seal*
*Pre Truman Administration*

*Presidential Seal*
*Post Truman Administration*

a gesture of war. Many presidents had redesigned the Great Seal. Franklin Delano Roosevelt had begun the process of redesign but had died before it was completed. Harry Truman continued with Roosevelt's plan and had the Eagle's head turned toward the olive branches. It remains this way today.

I tried to regain my balance and explained the history of my Opa's commission for the Harding Administration. I told him that the drawings had been approved by the White House.

He said, "How could they not pick up on that?" A question I certainly could not answer.

We ended our conversation pleasantly and talked about meeting for lunch on a day that never came.

*Seal of the President of the*
*United States*
*Door stop*
*The White House*

# *Chapter 7*
# *Residence of Mr. Del Coleman*

Helen Franklin Morton needed to design decorative iron gates for Del Colman's new residence. The well known Los Angeles interior decorator had undertaken the design phases for Coleman's new townhouse, 77 East 77th Street, on the northwest corner of Park Avenue and 77th Street.

We had a library of approximately three thousand period design

Hand forged & repoussé gate & fanlight

drawings. Franklin thumbed through them. It was as if she were picking from the menu of Chinese restaurant. She choose two sizes of rooster heads, forged scrolls, and repoussé leaves.

A *charrette* had been created. I was given the weekend to design the ensemble. There were two caveats: the design was not to be a copy, except for component parts and that we never use the design again.

I made sketches of different schemes and presented them to Frankin on Monday morning. She choose one and we began the commission.

After it was completed, I traveled to Europe on my one and only holiday for the next twenty years. I was studying ironwork, the proverbial "bus man's holiday." I wandered down a street in Florence and came upon an almost exact replica of Coleman's fanlight gates. But it was four hundred years old!

So was Ayn Rand right? I editorialize from *The Fountainhead*. "Twelve guys designed everything, after that, everything was a copy," This was put to music by Peter Allen and Carole Bayer Sager in the song "Everything Old Is New Again."

When I got back home, I called Franklin, told her about my discovery in Florence and listened to her laughter.

The library of designs that is mentioned in this chapter is available, free of charge, at **http://www.pafiebiger.com/**. The drawings are **not** copyright protected.

# *Chapter 8*
## *Brooke Astor's Residences*

**M**rs. Vincent Astor known as Brooke, was a most delightful person. Her larger- than-petite yet, smaller-than-large frame seemed to always be wearing a print dress. She often wore a floppy hat and white gloves.

Directoiré Stair Railing
Page Cross, Architect

When I first met her in 1967 she looked forty-five, not sixty-five. She was a combination of charm, grace, dignity, humility and beauty.

Page Cross was her friend and her architect. Jacqueline Kennedy's interior decorator for the Kennedy Era White House was the design firm Parish-Hadley. They also served Astor. Cross designed the Directoiré balustrade that is shown here. Albert Hadley and Sister Parish approved it.

Cold rolled steel did not exist in the late 19th century. Faithful to the late 19th century's Directoiré period, the balusters were machine tapered with iron rather than the now easily available, cold rolled steel. The decorative elements at the tops, bottoms and centers were cast in brass and gold plated. The handrail was lacquered walnut.

When Mabel Howard, Astor's mother died, Astor sold the upper floor and had us remove the railing and place it our storage area. A few years later, acting as her agent, we sold it to Rebekah Harkness.

In 1970, Cross designed entrance gates for the front and rear entrances of Astor's Briarcliff Manor in New York estate, *Holly Hill*. This stone manor was designed in 1927 by William Adams Delano for Dr. Hubert E. Rogers' estate called The Crossways. It had six marble fireplaces and thirteen bedrooms. The curved stair had a delicate forged iron railing made by Opa and Dad. They also made the repoussé Espalier Tree motif garden gate and forged trellis assembly for the porch adjacent to the sun room.

Driveway gates, pedestrian gates, fieldstone piers, lighting fixtures and all of the accoutrements that go into estate portals were required. Cross and I took the prototype of the gate to Briarcliff Manor for Astor's approval.

I had made other day trips with Cross, so I was only a little nervous this time. He made me at ease as we chatted. I knew he cared about me. He said, "I've watched you grow up, Joe. Are you enjoying the business?"

"I'm not so scared anymore, but I sure was for a while."

"I knew that, I liked that about you, don't change."

We were silent for a few moments, I broke the silence with, "Mr.

Cross, my Dad had a funny blush on prototypes. He used to say, 'Never show a fool half a job.'"

"I really liked your father."

"He liked you a lot too," I replied.

"I heard him say that at the Church once. He's probably right, but we have no choice. Besides, Brooke is nobody's fool."

As we continued on what Cross called our "motor trip," he told me how he had explained the costs relating to this work to Astor. The scope of work encompassed driveway gates for the front and service entrances. The main entrance had four stone columns, a pedestrian gate, fence, lighting fixtures and an announcement system. Site preparation was extensive. Concrete foundations were poured to the frost line. Reinforced concrete columns that encapsulated structural steel to support the gates were poured. Stone masons cut indigenous blocks and set them on the concrete surface. Telephone and electrical services were installed.

Astor asked Cross if he was sure that he had prepared for the future. He replied. "We've hired the best security firms in New York. We're state of the art."

"Well, Page," she asked, "how much do you think that this project will cost?" Cross told her he thought that it would be between $300,000 and $400,000.

He imitated her voice rather well and said, voice rising, "I'll have to sell my money."

"Money?"

Voice still rising, she said, "Monet, Page! My Monet! I'll have to sell a Monet!"

He was laughing as he wound the tale down.

Always gracious, Brooke Astor invited us in for tea before inspecting the prototype. We entered through the vestibule into the grand marble foyer. I was overcome! Here stood Dad and Opa's railing from 1927. I had seen the drawings in our files, the photos, even the prototypes and the extra parts, but I had never seen the actual railing. This was not the first time that this had happened. Each time, I cherished it.

We sat for tea. Social grace and business. Astor wanted to discuss a strange development that had played out. The home owner, though allowed to protect himself from intruders was not allowed to inflict harm on that intruder. There had been a case in New York where an intruder who attempted to scale a picket fence had become impaled and lost a finger. We were aware of this still-blooming undercurrent and designed the pickets to "break away" under stress. We decided that the alloy and design should be highlighted on our drawings and passed on to the insurance carrier. "Discretion," we agreed, "was the better part of valor."

More tea was served. I was relaxed and enjoyed our meeting when Astor, serious, yet of soft voice, she said to me, "Joe dear, do you like dogs?"

I replied honestly that had no experiences with them. She continued, "I could never trust a man who did not like dogs."

I had no reply, save for a rather sheepish smile. Luckily, she already liked me, liked our work and the status quo was maintained.

Driving back to the city, Cross told me that Astor had bequeathed the estate to the Catholic Church so that the Nuns could have a pleasant retreat. Approximately thirty-five years later it played out sadly. Her bequest was contested by her son and the estate was sold on the real estate market. Years later, forced to relocate to the Southwest, I fell in love with dogs.

Thanks, Mrs. Astor.

# *Chapter 9*
# *21 Club*

One of the most famous restaurants in American history is the 21 Club. Opened by cousins Jack Kreindler and Charles Berns in Greenwich Village in 1922, it came to rest at 21 West 52nd Street in 1929 as *Jack and Charlie's 21*.

It was a speakeasy during prohibition. They had an elaborate system of levers and pulleys that swept the liquor away in the blink of an eye.

Opa and Dad designed and executed all of the ironwork for the building. They supervised the design and casting of the famous jockeys and installed them in a manner that would prevent pilferage.

Every year the club painted the jockeys the silk colors of the horses that competed in the Kentucky Derby. My father said that after a few years

21 Club

the paint became too thick and they were commissioned to remove it.

The ironwork and jockeys were the hallmark of the club. At Christmas, the club commissioned famous designers to design scarves with the ironwork and jockeys as the motif.

Jerry Berns whose name was obviously not in the original moniker lobbied to have the name changed to "21." I met Berns when I was a boy and enjoyed our casual relationship for years.

Something at the restaurant or the warehouse always needed attention.

He was always gracious and, as you would imagine, literate in every field. One day he and I were discussing the Yankees. Not the game, not the players, not the press – the owners.

"Mr. Berns," I asked, "what makes you guys so special?"

He didn't even blink. "Great food and being nice to everybody."

He called one day with a large problem. They needed a new staircase in the kitchen.

We did not make staircases, just as we did not do the jockeys. Berns knew this, but he wanted our involvement because of our attention to detail.

He said, "You only have two days to take out the old and put in the new one. Can you do it?"

"I guess it just has to be done."

"We'll be closed for the Memorial Day weekend. Do it then."

There were other special requirements.

The new stair had to be wider than the one it was replacing. Waiters had to be able to pass each other without collision. There was ample room to accomplish this.

The stair also had to muffle the footfalls of the staff and it had to have non-slip treads. Most importantly, it had to be able to be washed down every night.

I called the brothers Oderwald, friends of my father, at Stephen

Oderwald, Inc. They were structural steel and miscellaneous iron fabricators who performed fine work. I explained the parameters. Naturally, an all aluminum stair was needed.

Les and Ray Oderwald met me at 21 with their draftsmen and the process began. They figured out the soundproofing and waterproofing details.

At seven o'clock on the Saturday morning of Memorial Day weekend, trucks and men arrived at 21. I was with Berns to meet them.

They had the old stair cut apart and out of the building by ten o'clock. The area was swept and hosed down. Installation of the new stair began.

A skeleton crew of kitchen staff offered coffee and pastries to the men. They drank and they ate, but they never stopped working.

A little past lunch time the stringers had been set, the non-slip treads were in place, and the major body of work had been completed. This was going so well that Berns decided that he was no longer needed. As he left, he whispered something to a chef.

The chef, his tall white hat standing upright, asked the foreman, "Are you guys hungry?"

"We brought our lunches with us."

"Would you like something a little different?"

This got everybody's attention. "Like what?"

"Many of the clientele of 21 are hunters. They often have their game sent to the club and kept in the freezer. Sometime later I prepare their catch for them."

Freezer inventory was running high.

"I have pheasant that the boss wants me to get rid of. Would you guys like Pheasant? I'll make it *en gelée*."

"*En gelée?*"

"Under glass, a glaze."

"Are you joking?"

"No, I'll make it for you if you guys are sure you'll finish by tomorrow night."

"Tomorrow night? We'll be finished in a few hours."

The aura of, "is he kidding," had gone. The men anticipated the banquet with great delight. When the risers and treads were installed, the chef called everyone to dine.

The masterpiece luncheon was served on the large table where employees ate. Everyone washed and joked that they needed neckties. The pheasant was displayed on a silver serving dish. The flatware and china were pedestrian. Bread, salad and wine accompanied the meal. The chef wrapped the uneaten pheasant in a wax like paper, and put it in brown bags for the men to take home. What fun it was.

By seven o'clock the project was completed. It was safe, soundproof and waterproof.

Berns called at 6:30 Tuesday morning to express his thanks. I thanked him on behalf of the men, for lunch.

I had never dined, at 21. Berns knew this. "Joe, are you married?" He asked.

"No, not yet."

"Anybody in mind?"

"I'm enjoying being a playboy. Plus, I work all the time."

"When you do get married, call me. I'll treat you and your bride to dinner."

I have still never dined at 21. When I was married seven years later, I thought about calling him, but I just couldn't do it.

# Chapter 10
## Enid Haupt's Residences

Enid Haupt liked to say, "Nature is my religion." For more than fifty years, her greatest joys were sharing her religion. A principal beneficiary was the New York Botanical Garden in the Bronx.

She was one of eight children born in Milwaukee to Sadie and Moses Annenberg. He made the family fortune publishing *The Philadelphia Inquirer*, *The Philadelphia Daily News*, *The Daily Racing Form*, *TV Guide* and radio and television. They comprised some of the holdings of Triangle Publications. Haupt as editor-in-chief, later added *Seventeen Magazine* to the corporate mix.

Seventy-one east Seventy-first Street, the side entrance to 740 Park Avenue, is one of Manhattan's most prestigious apartment buildings. The multitalented Steven Candela was the architect.

The original staircases and railings that he designed throughout the building were all the same. Circular stair cases were made with marble and an iron balustrade with a polished bronze handrail. The motif was a full "S" with a vertical arrow passing through it. The arrow had polished bronze extremities. For all intense and purposes, it was a dollar sign.

I wondered if Candela was poking fun at his clients when he designed this. Other noted artists and artisans have left subtle messages for their patrons.

Haupt and I were discussing her design schemes for the renovation of her new apartment. She hired neither architect nor designer. She had these skills and she used them.

I took the liberty of asking her what she saw when she looked at the railing. I detailed my query about the motif being a folly. "Others have done it, Piazza Navona, the Biltmore," I said.

She looked at me with bemusement and offered a rare and pleasant

*Louis XVI hand forged & repoussé stair railing*
*New York City Residence*
*Designed by Jean Balbous & Joseph Fiebiger*

smile. "I don't think he was playing with John D. Rockefeller, Jr.," she said.

"Mrs. Haupt," I said, "my father changed Rockefeller's stair railings many years ago."

Her glasses had slid down her nose, she looked over them, offering a pleasant and forgiving smile. At sixty-one, sharp featured and lithe, Haupt was an alert, stunning women. "Did Hunt do that to Vanderbilt at the Bilt-more?" She asked.

"I doubt that it was Hunt. I think that the artisans just got bored with the repetitive panels and decided to turn one around. Just folly."

"Cute, but academic, I don't like this one. I want a railing like the one at the Wildenstein Gallery. I'll take you there."

The next day we visited Mr. Wildenstein at his famous gallery on 64th Street. The stair railing was magnificent. I studied it while she talked with Wildenstein. She called to me, "I don't want you to copy this, I want you to make a better one." I saw her wink at Wildenstein.

"No one could make one any better than this, " I said.

We had a set of full size drawings, painted in oils by the well known French stair builder, the late Jean Balbous. He and my father had designed a railing that had never been made. I told Haupt that the intended client had been Samuel Reichmann.

She sparkled. "Where are the paintings?"

"In the office."

We got in her limousine and were off to the shop. She climbed the spiral stair to the office with great care. I was worried about getting her mink coat dirty; she was concerned about her balance.

The motif revealed itself before I finished unrolling the paintings. She peeked. "I love it. Please, make it."

She took one of the paintings home and had it temporarily mounted on a wall.

Months before he died, Dad managed to visit Haupt's apartment and inspect the railing. He looked at it, walked around it, touched it, and cried. Haupt bore silent witness to our event and graciously gave us our privacy.

Dad felt well enough to drive home. As we wound our way up the Henry Hudson Parkway he took  my hand, "I'm proud of you, Joe.  I love you."

Still to this day, once a day, I hold out my left hand and feel his love. I use a special hug for Mom.

A few years later Haupt bought a house in Palm Beach. Again, she used her own talents to modify the architecture and interior design. She had seen the Directoiré railing that we made for Mrs. Astor, and loved it. She wanted to transform it from period French to modern.

We designed tapered balusters with unadorned, turned fittings. The shafts were made of polished stainless steel while the fittings were turned in brass and gold plate.

She mixed her architectural metaphors often. We used an eclectic

*Modern stair railing*
*Palm Beach Residence*
*Designed by Joseph Fiebiger*

blend of forgings and repoussé leaves to fashion two false perspective sky-lights.

I followed her philanthropic endeavors and was proud to have known her. I enjoyed our fleeting relationship.

*Hand forged & repoussé skylight*
*Palm Beach Residence*
*Designed by Joseph Fiebiger*

The creation of Central Park began in 1858. Most of the landscapes were completed twenty years later. Five hundred thousand cubic feet of topsoil were carted in from New Jersey. Workers dug by hand. More than ten million cart loads of materials and debris were carted in and out with horse-drawn carts. Five hundred thousand trees were planted. Thirty-six bridges and arches were built. Six man made bodies of water, fed from upstate New York were created. The entire park, 843 acres, was man made.

William Cullen Bryant, editor of the *Evening Post,* joined with landscape gardener and publisher of *The Horticulturist* magazine, Andrew Jackson Downing, in 1844 to campaign for land to be set aside for a large public park in Manhattan. Developers were accumulating land parcels as the city's development moved quickly. What must be considered truly remarkable, city politicians agreed and

Bow Bridge
Central Park

both parties consented to endorse the idea of a large public park.

In 1857 an independent board of commissioners sponsored a public competition. Thirty-three entrants proposed plans for the new park. The *Greensward* plan was the collaborative work of Frederick Law Olmsted, thirty-five, and Calvert Vaux, thirty-three. Vaux was the British architect who had originally convinced the commissioners to hold a design competition.

The design of Central Park embraced Olmsted's social consciousness. He believed that a common green space must always be equally accessible to all citizens. One of Olmsted's humanitarian accomplishments was the creation of the Sanitary Commission, precursor to the Red Cross, during the Civil War.

Bow Bridge is said by some to be named for its resemblance to an archer's bow. It is located mid park at 74th Street, west of Bethesda Terrace. It connects Cherry Hill and the Ramble and was designed by Vaux and Jacob Wrey Mould. Though it is the second oldest cast iron bridge in the United States, it was designed to mimic limestone. Thirteen years later Vaux and Mould were the first architects of the Metropolitan Museum of Art. Unfortunately their building was disliked.

The bridge was manufactured by the iron foundry known in 1858 as Janes and Beebe, known a few years later as Janes, Fowler and Kirtland. History does not tell us the fates of Messrs. Beebe or Fowler, but Janes, Kirtland & Company became the moniker. Their offices were on Reade Street in Manhattan. The foundry encompassed a few square blocks in the Morrisania section of the Bronx.

In the latter part of the 1850s, Janes and Beebe won a contract to fabricate the cast iron plates for the inner and outer shells of the new United States Capitol dome, designed by Thomas U. Walter.

The cast iron of the 1860s was known to be strong in compression, yet its strength in tension still awaited approval. Therefore it was used as cladding with major structural support provided by structural steel. Henry Bessemer had patented his steel making process in 1855. Steel was now 1,000 times stronger than iron.

We certainly know the designers of the bridge, yet those who engineered it are an enigma. The engineers designed a steel plate box or beam system to support the bridge. This method was used twenty-five years later in subway girder construction. Steel plates, nominally forty-eight inches wide and ninety-eight inches long were riveted to two inch angle iron, one quarter of an inch thick. These iron members were riveted at right angles to the upper and lower quarter of inch thick plates. During our restoration I heard very prominent engineers animatedly debate if the structure is in fact a "box" or a "beam." They could never agree. The iron castings that decorate the bridge were attached to steel plates with flat head machine screws. There were no expansion joints.

One school of thought was that the mechanical connections allowed the pieces to be free to react to constant oscillation and expansion and contraction.

Though she may have derived her name from an archer's bow, some believed that she was designed radially, with a bow, to provide additional strength and to allow for thermal movement. Not only were cast iron's properties of compression and tension being studied, so were its coefficients of expansion and contraction. An arch allowed unrestricted movement. A second precaution was taken as they built the side near the ramble on cast iron cannon balls. Now it could move up and down as well as forward and backward. This was explained in the *1860-1865 Commissioner's Report*.

One hundred and ten years later, we hired a diver to brave the murky water. He didn't find them.

Cast iron through the end of the Civil War, had a deadly percentage of phosphorus. It allowed for the material to be viscous and produce thin elements. Exposure to the vapors however, caused necrosis of the bones in the jaw. Folklore has it that many foundry workers suffered similarly to the mercury poisoning of the "Mad Hatters."

The presence of phosphorus was of great concern to us. Original castings that some thought should be replaced anew, could not be. The 19th century castings were five-sixteenths of an inch thick. Twentieth century pieces were five-eights of an inch thick which was twice the thickness, twice the weight.

Thankfully, no one even suggested using aluminum. That would have violated every rule of a faithful restoration and would have set up electromotive forces that would have been deleterious.

Eutectic Corporation, a world leader in welding technology was consulted. They had a welding rod with exceptionally high nickel content, a proprietary recipe that would work. We welded with these rods, covered the welds with hot coals and allowed them to cool slowly. The process worked very well.

Cast iron is not supposed to rust. Usually it *blooms* and then arrests itself. Yet under extreme circumstances, cast iron will rust. It has its place in the nobility of metals and sacrifices itself to protect more noble metals. Handrail and baseboard moldings that had been cast and were the most severely corroded were replaced with iron reproductions. Castings that needed to be repaired had their afflicted areas cut away. Those pieces were cast anew. Because they were small, the foundry was able to get a thickness of approximately three eighths of an inch. We fit them to the originals with flat head machine screws, using back up plates called *Dutchmen*. The joints were welded and baked.

Two female philanthropists had been the major benefactors of the project. Mrs. Lucy Moses whose husband, Henry had founded the law firm of Moses & Singer, was also a noted banker. Mrs. Lila Acheson Wallace was cofounder with her husband, DeWitt, of the Reader's Digest. This was a "girls night out" thing. A third lady joined the team, the always-ready-to-help Brooke Astor.

The restoration of Bow Bridge was the beginning of the restoration era in the park. It had a high profile, and was watched by many. Success here would open the way for future projects. Parks, Recreation and Cultural Affairs personnel prepared for the dedication. Not uncommon, a piece of graffiti in the famous four letter "F" expletive had been painted prominently on a very large rock near the entrance to the bridge. PRCA issued a work order to have it sandblasted away. But they didn't tell the operator to blast the whole rock. He only blasted away the four characters. Comedy or tragedy, laugh or cry, there were many wry smiles.

Before we began the commission I had consulted with our insurance carrier of many, many years, General Accident. One of their vice-presidents, our agent, a lifetime friend of my father's and I went to see the bridge and have lunch. While eating, the VP suggested that we not take this commission because he thought that *they* were at risk. My blood boiled, but I said nothing. No sense spoiling a good Monte Crisco sandwich. When I returned to the office I called a friend in the insurance business and began the process of changing carriers.

We had embarked upon this commission as joint venture with my good friend and builder Richard Hanington of William Crawford, Inc. Dick handled all of the general construction phases, we did the ironwork. When completed, the accounting revealed that we had barely broken even and Dick made a $10,000 profit. He said, "You did all the work, it's yours."

The ornamental fountain at Cherry Hill was designed by Vaux and Mold, but was never made. Approximately one hundred and ten years later, Central Park Conservancy's director, Elizabeth Barlow wanted to make it. I asked her about it

Cherry Hill Fountain
Central Park

years later. She said, "Well, better late than never."

She charged historical architect Gerald Allen with tasks of executing the wishes of the original architects. He was commissioned to restore the *cul de sac* in the park. A major feature was the creation of a 19th century fountain for 20th century use. He added electrical fixtures and enhanced the water chalices to provide drinking water for the horses.

It was always a privilege to shake historical hands with the creators of Central Park.

The Carousel, which had been a fixture in the park since 1871, was destroyed by fire and replaced in the fall of 1950. It is said to have the largest hand carved horses anywhere in the world.

The Ehrenkrantz Group was awarded the commission to design new fences that would enclose the Carousel.

The lead architect, Jean Parker Murphy incorporated a frieze with two styles of horses in different gaits, shown by the positions of their legs.

Fred Helbing of A-1 Flushing Pattern Works, commissioned an equestrian wood carver to make the patterns. Gender was never discussed.

The carvings were exquisite. The gaits were right, but the carver had given each horse a gender. There were "boy" horses and there were "girl" horses.

A very observant child, waiting entrance to the Merry Go Round could certainly discern the difference. This was an "Oh My God!" moment.

Thankfully, death by hanging was ruled out. I was safe. But there was a "delicate" problem that needed a remedy. There were many off color comments, some humorous. But none offered a solution. Gender or genderless? That was the question.

Their perfect gaits were maintained; the horses were rendered genderless.

# Chapter 12
## Caramoor Center For Music & The Arts
## Katonah, New York

International financier Walter Tower Rosen and his wife Luci created Caramoor in Katonah, New York in 1928. The Rosen's were passionate in their collection of art, and their devotion to music.

Many architectural elements were purchased in Europe and brought to Katonah to mix with this Moorish flavor. A set of iron gates, circa 1780, was imported from Switzerland, another a pair was imported from Spain. The Swiss gates are at the entrance to the theatre while the Spanish gates protect the courtyard.

Opa had been commissioned in 1928 to adapt the Swiss gates,

18th Century Swiss Gates after 1975 restoration

fabricate side panels with lanterns and install the assembly. They had been set in a Chapel and were in good condition.

The Spanish gates demonstrated the history of ironwork in different parts of Europe. The vertical bars were sandwiched between two horizontal members, fastened via rivets. Artisans in France, Germany and Italy always passed the vertical bars through a horizontal bar that had been pierced to allow the passage, which was a much more precise and labor intense procedure.

In 1975 the Swiss gates were held in place by habit and old paint. Restoration was mandated. The Spanish gates also needed attention, but they were not in danger of failure.

The restoration of the Swiss gates began with photographs and dimensional drawings. Anne Stern, daughter of the Rosen's and Michael Sweeley, Director of Caramoor, wanted the original elements of the work preserved.

We were instructed to save everything and introduce no new iron unless absolutely necessary. We soaked the gates with a mild paint remover and then lightly micro blasted away the remover and the rust. None of the iron was removed. Decayed iron was *repuddled*. We heated it to welding heat (2200 degrees Fahrenheit) and allowed new iron to atomically bond with the old via puddling. There were some places where new material had to be introduced for structural value. The original iron forgings that we saved comprised the motif and had the initials of the artisans who had made them. They also had part numbers in Roman Numerals incised.

We used modern technology, made the pivoting mechanisms with stainless steel, used ball bearings and *oilite* bronze bushings. The gates operated with the ease of a baby carriage.

An organic zinc finishing system with a total of eight mils was applied. This thinness of paint allowed the initials and Roman numerals to not be lost.

The original artisans naturally used all of the techniques of their era. In the mid 18th century welding was done as *forge welding*. Two pieces of iron were brought to *snowball heat*. The iron spit off white sparks in excess of 2350 degrees Fahrenheit. A flux, sometimes as simple as baking soda, was applied to shield the oxygen. These artisans were proficient at this task but they could not keep the welded assemblies square. All the heat and the hammering forced the assemblies to wander. The gates and the scroll work were out of square. Obviously, being out of square they could be neither plumb nor square.

I presented this issue to Stern and Sweeley and the debate began. Our 20th century skills allowed us to easily correct this situation. We could

Hand forged stair railing
Mott B. Schmidt, Architect

46

adjust the convolution of the scrolls with the use of *gabels* or bending forks and we could set the joinery of the gates. These adjustments would park the scrolls in a tangent posture, square to the frame and make the gates square. But should we?

I posed the question, "As 20th century artisans, are we allowed to use the technology of our era? If these 18th century men had this technology they would have used it," I argued.

We could have cheated in the installation process to assure that out-of-square gates behaved as plumb gates and didn't either open or close on their own.

This was an all or nothing procedure. We could not perform it and make it reversible.

After considerable debate Stern and Sweeley deemed it acceptable for 20th century technology to be used to render more precise an 18th century architectural masterpiece.

Stern and Sweeley commissioned the highly acclaimed architect Mott B. Schmidt to design a new extension to the original building. Schmidt, an octogenarian, had recently recovered from a stroke. A right handed man, he taught himself to draw with his left hand to design this new wing.

Schmidt's signature piece of his work was the "Flying Staircase." I had the privilege to help him design the stair railings for his last grand circular stair.

## *Chapter 13*
## *Rebekah Harkness' Residence and Theatre*

Rebekah Harkness was a grand dame of the ballet and a philanthropist. Her second marriage was to Standard Oil heir William Hale Harkness. They were a happy couple and enjoyed collaborating on musical scores. He died seven years into the marriage and bequeathed his estate to her, their child and children from their previous marriages. She enjoyed the burdens and glories associated with her social status for the next forty years. Her largess benefited the William Hale Harkness Pavilion at New York Hospital and numerous other foundations until her death in 1982 at the age of sixty-seven.

Married several times, she never found a mate equal to Harkness.

In 1967 Harkness purchased the seven-and-a-half acre estate of movie legend Katherine Cornell. The wooded grounds overlooked the Hudson River in Sneden's Landing, New York. The interior design team of Florence Clark and Rafa Varga were hired as interior decorators.

Varga did watercolor sketches of his ideas. He gave them to me for implementation into stair railings and grilles. He wanted to make stair railings with decorative bronze elements that he called Cartouchés. We played with the designs, a bow, its angle set to the angle of the stair, with ribbons that terminated in tassels as they touched the stair tread. At the midpoint was a page of music and 19th century musical instruments. The page was the size of the center-to-center dimension of two stair treads. The newel posts were of crystal with bronze acanthus leaf bases and baccarat crystal finials.

Harkness, Clark and Varga arrived at the shop in her classic, powder blue Rolls Royce. All work in the shop stopped when they entered the building. Harkness was a beautiful lady with long flowing blonde hair and a lithe yet powerful figure. When we met she smiled and said, "I have heard only good things about you? They were right, you are handsome. Can I call you Joe?"

I blushed, "Of course."

Varga introduced her to the men. She shook each man's hand and accepted the offer of a cup of coffee. "Milk, no sugar."

I took her hand and escorted her to the spiral stair that led to the

*Louis XVI stair railing for grand circular stair*
*bronze cartouchés, bronze acanthus leaf ornaments and*
*Baccarate crystal with polished bronze handrail*
*Sneden's Landing, NY Residence*
*Designed by Rafa Varga and Joseph Fiebiger*
*Ca. 1968*

office. She navigated the difficult stair with grace. Varga had lingered in the shop, talking as he liked to do, in Spanish with Perez. He was the last to close the door from the shop to the stair hall. The work resumed and the cacophony of the hammers filtered their way to the office.

Once in the office, she said, "Is that the sound of your work? That's some pulse. It's music." Her eyes darted to the wall where a full size drawing of the Cartouché was hung. Her face lit up.

She asked Varga, "Can the lines of my musical score be placed on the page?"

He looked to me. I nodded.

Everyone smiled. Then Harkness asked me, "Will it be very hard to make this railing so that it is perfect? I want it to be as good as those in Versailles."

"We'll make it and install it, then take it down, make adjustments and re-install it."

"That should do it. I like that idea."

I walked them outside. Harkness took me by the elbow and guided me to the front of the car. The hood ornament was the traditional one for Rolls Royce. She said, "Can you make my 'little man' to replace this?"

I looked to Varga. He interrupted, "Joe, Rebekah has a symbol of the ballet that Salvador Dali designed for her. Its the figure of a male dancing figure. He is reading a book held high above his head with a branch of leaves attached to each foot. Its on all the china at Harkness House." He turned to Harkness, "Can we give him a plate?"

She nodded and guided me to the

rear door of the car where the figure was very tastefully painted under the window.

"We can make this. Gold plated, I assume. It's going to be harder to figure out how to spring load it than to make it."

The chauffeur had overheard. He grabbed me gently by my arm, "I wash this car," he said with pride, "It never goes to car washes. It'll be safe with me."

We had the Cartouchés cast in bronze and chased them. They were beautiful and commanded attention. We installed the railing for the main stair. Harkness and everyone else, loved it. She decided to replicate it for railings in the music room and her boudoir.

*Hand forged & repoussé grilles for
entrance doors
Sneden's Landing, NY residence
Designed by Joseph Fiebiger
Ca. 1968*

One cold April day Perez and I were on our haunches, installing the railing in her living quarters . He was smoking a cigar as he worked. Harkness had been swimming, *au naturel*, in her heated pool . She glided into the room wearing only a mink coat. She smiled at me, dropped the coat, and walked into the bedroom. The cigar fell from Perez' mouth. He muttered *"Dios mío, José."* I was too scared to follow.

Thankfully the moment passed. Harkness, not at all disturbed, went on into her dressing room.

I unfolded the story for Dad in the evening. He laughed and said, "Its a good thing you didn't follow her. If  you were lousy lay, we would have lost a good job." Mom, heard this from the kitchen and joined the laughter.

The residence was about three quarters completed in August 1968. The interior decoration phase waited for purple fabric to be woven in Paris for the wall coverings. The shipment arrived and was installed just in time for an important social event.

Harkness was having a luncheon for her ballet troupe. The guest of honor was First Lady, Lady Bird Johnson. Every detail was attended to with great attention.

The entourage arrived first, followed by the grand entrance of Mrs. Johnson. As they mingled, the morning grew warm, then hot. Harkness instructed the maid, Pasquale, to turn on the air conditioning.

"*Oui*, madame," She ran to find the switch, and returned dismayed. "Madam, where is the switch?"

"I don't know.  Ask Cook"

"*Oui*, madam"

No one could find the switch for the air conditioning. The day was getting hotter and the customary breezes off the Hudson were lazy. Harkness was steaming. She asked for her telephone book and called the home of the principal in the architectural firm.

"How do you turn on the air conditioning system?"

"What air conditioning system? You didn't tell us to air condition the house."

I heard many versions of this story, but one thing was the same in each. The festivities were not harmed by the lack of temperature control. Fortunately a summer storm came down from Bear Mountain and chilled the air.

Harkness ordered the architect to air condition the house. This now took on the flavor of a "Keystone Cops" movie. Tradesmen worked at breakneck speed to install traditional through-the-wall air conditioners.

Laugh or to cry? When the air conditioners were turned on they introduced uncontrolled humidity. As the windows sweated, yards and yards of purple fabric bled.

Next spring a de-humidification system was installed. Damaged carpets and wall coverings were replaced. Varga explained, "She has a way of accepting little set backs with grace and then moving on."

We continued with more railings, door grilles, kitchen pot racks and spiral stairs for the studio.

I saw Harkness next in the late spring of '69 in the new music room. Dad had died in March. She and many other patrons had sent their condolences and floral arrangements. She asked, "Are you okay? How's your Mom?"

"Even when you know its coming, it's not easy. Mom's as okay as she can be, I guess. Thanks for the flowers. Thanks for asking."

"How long are you going to wear that black tie?" She asked.

"Maybe forever."

"Time will heal that. The love will stay, but the pain will go. You'll take it off when you feel right about it."

"Its nice of you to care."

The music room was an enchanted space. About to leave, she stopped abruptly, looked around, smiled with open arms and said, "Thanks for making so many beautiful things. I appreciate all that you and your men did."

Harkness wanted to have a theatre. Her theatre--her ballet. She purchased the former R.K.O. Colonial movie theatre at Broadway and Sixty-Second Street, slightly east of Lincoln Center. Architect Stanley Grant was hired to effect the building's transition. His paramount responsibility was to create the best possible work space for the dancers as well as provide a pleasant sight line.

Harkness had decided to allow her muralist, Enrique Oliver-Senis, to wear two hats. He was be the interior designer and the artist. He painted a spirited collection of nude dancers, seemingly at play on the proscenium arch. He worked á la Michelangelo. Save for the facts that he had a refrigerator, music, a climate controlled workspace on the scaffolding and a six-way electric front seat, replete with battery, from a 1968 Ford Thunderbird.

I always thought of him as Desi in the "I Love Lucy" TV show. He was built like Desi, but he often acted like Lucy. Nonetheless, he was a friendly fellow. I visited him in his arena, high above the theatre to discuss our progress on various aspects of the work. He suggested a break and lunch at the much heralded O'Neals Balloon. He said, "Will you do me a favor after lunch? Will you drive me to a bank on Madison Avenue?"

"Of course."

We got in one of the company trucks that I used to get around Manhattan. Snow was falling and the temperature was dropping. I drove across town and pulled up in front of the bank. Normally one drives around the block. Parking on Madison Avenue is prohibited.

Senis said, "Wait here. I won't be long."

I sat in the truck for a while and sure enough, a patrolman approached and bellowed, "Move it, Pal." The storm was more intense. I drove around the block. As I made the turn back onto Madison, the bank was still a block away. Through the snow I saw a man I thought was Senis. He was running, and he was limping.

I had visions of "Bonnie and Clyde." What had this guy done? He grabbed the door handle and thrust himself into the truck. His face was red and he was winded, but he was not scared. Good, I wasn't aiding and abetting.

"What happened?"

"I took out ten thousand dollars and put it in my shoe."

I laughed. "Why didn't you put five in each foot?"

*Orchestra railing without decorative swags*
*Ca. 1974*

"I should have thought of that," he said, as he removed both shoes and redistributed his cash.

Senis was smart to copy Varga's designs. He used the Cartouchés and designed swags between them for the orchestra railing.

Brooke Astor's mother had died and she was reverting the apartment to simplex. We had disassembled the Directoiré railing and were holding the balusters in storage. I told Senis about the balusters over lunch. He asked me to approach Astor and ask if she would sell them to Harkness.

I told all of this to Page Cross, Astor's architect and friend. He pushed the right buttons and Astor sold the balusters to Harkness. We used them to make a straight railing that led to the mezzanine.

We made three sets of entrance doors to the theatre. The grilles had an eclectic French Provençal flavor, forged scrolls and, gilded repoussé leaves.

My wife Balinda and I were invited to the opening night of the ballet. Harkness wearing her nine-hundred-thousand dollar diamond tiara, was accompanied by First Lady, Betty Ford. The air conditioning system worked fine. But even though they were followed by Pinkerton and Secret Service, social snipers were at work.

Some said that there was antipathy between Harkness and *New York Times* critic, Clive Barnes. He was unmerciful with his review of the ballet and the theatre's architecture. He said, "I have never seen its match in flamboyance or . . . vulgarity." The modern ballet performed that night was crucified in similar fashion.

Perhaps the vulgarity here was vested in Barnes himself. His comment, "It was like watching the Titanic sink," may have been true in his eyes.

Yet Harkness' munificent deeds went unsaluted during the ambush.

As Varga had said years before, she rebounded quickly and moved on. Luckily for the recipients of her largess, these episodes never halted her philanthropy.

Harkness' estate had endowed two foundations that merged to the Harkness Foundation For Dance. Under the guidance of Theodore S. Bartwink, it makes about two hundred grants a year, totalling over $1.25 million dollars a year.

My father gave credit to patrons likes Harkness for the survival of the artisans during the Depression. He said, "They took a page out Lorenzo de' Medici's book."

Rebekah Harkness, albeit on a smaller scale, was cast in the mold of Lorenzo de' Medici.

# Chapter 15
## Gainesway Farm, Lexington, KY

John R. Gaines was born into the Gaines Dog Food Company family. He was a leader in the National Thoroughbred Racing Association and founder of the Breeder's Cup. In 1962, thirty-three years old, he established Gainesway Farm in Lexington, Kentucky. In 1978 he hired Theodore M. Ceraldi to be the architect and asked him to design a transformation of the rolling hills of his 1500 acre farm to an equestrian palace. This was based on a four stall barn for thoroughbred stallions

Ceraldi was successful. Gainesway Farm was noted as an architectural masterpiece for the thoroughbred world and received a National AIA Award for excellence in architecture. Ceraldi was an architect with the soul of a poet. His designs were a combination poet and realist.

Ceraldi designed iron gates, fences, doors, hardware, and farm equipment that were always a challenge. What else was new? The sliding gates for the horses' barns were metaphorical horses. The motif was the abstract frontal view of a horse. Naturally he chose a method of joinery that was extremely difficult to execute with precision--fifteen thousand of these joints were required.

Once again, the brilliance of Master Craftsmen Gennaro Ranieri found viable methods to achieve Ceraldi's goals. He and another talented craftsmen, Joe Karhut, collaborated on a scheme in which these joints could be flattened with precision in a specific area and pierced simultaneously. They used water to quench the iron and reduce the arithmetic creep that always revealed its ugly head. One problem was solved.

Next, the gates had to be silent when operated. These "kings of kings" could not get "spooked" by a squeak, grind or squeal. The gates also had to be strong, beautiful, and secure. Rollers of this type did not exist commercially. We designed an iron track upon which would ride very special trucks, wheels and axles. We had to minimize friction while still providing linear motion.

Fred Helbing made wood patterns of the wheels. We planned to experiment by casting them in a special bronze alloy that is used to make bearings and bushings. The trade name for this material is *oilite bronze*. This is a very porous texture that absorbs and holds oil. We had them cast, machined and then soaked in oil for two weeks. The experiment worked well. The wheels did not squeak

Ceraldi had introduced me to his uncle, Ed Onny. Onny was a principal of LORS Machinery. The firm designed and manufactured specialized welding equipment. Onny thought that they could manufacture

Forged Gates
Theordore Ceraldi, Architect

58

an electric forge that would heat iron quicker than our conventional coal forge. Not only could they produce the heat, they could attach two hydraulic cylinders that would allow us to either push or pull the iron. Almost like pulling or pushing taffy. The consummate gentlemen, Onny offered to make the machine and stipulated that if it failed, he would take it back.

We tried the machine and it was magic. We placed iron bars as large as one inch square in the hydraulic/electric jaws. The iron reached 2,200 degrees Fahrenheit quickly. The jaws did indeed push the hot iron in on itself, a process in blacksmithery called *upsetting*. It also allowed the iron to stretch and thin out.

But when we placed a piece of curved iron in the jaws, the iron burned up, sparked white, and vanished before our eyes. None of us had remembered that electricity always takes the path of least resistance. In this case, that path was across the arc of the spiral, not around it.

We were all disappointed. Onny, true to his word, took the machine back. He did not bemoan the ill fortune. It was good experiment. We all learned from our mistake.

Odd how things work out. A few years later, when confronted with a calamitous problem at the Statue of Liberty, I called upon Onny's genius to help find a solution. Onny sold us ninety thousand dollars worth of equipment and was allowed to put his company nameplate on this electric annealing machines. Thousands of visitors were able to witness it turn a cold, dark bar of stainless steel to the white heat of 1905 degrees Fahrenheit.

I had developed a friendship with Ceraldi. John Gaines was a very personable, warm man, easy to like. It was fun to share stories, usually over coffee. As we chatted we sketched on napkins, place mats and sometimes even table cloths. Successful meetings were judged by how many napkins and placements we went through.

I was invited to watch the actual breeding of exceptional stallions. This is a very special event. The Thoroughbred Association attends this, as do veterinarians and technicians. I thought that I was watching a Woody Allen movie. I stood quietly in a group with Gaines, Ceraldi, Joe Taylor, their famous manager. The mood was so deadly serious that it was almost comical. Video cameras taped the proceedings. Big money was at stake here, but it was surreal nonetheless.

Almost Aryan, this quest for perfection--hoping and betting against regression to the mean. The stallion was teased to become sexually aroused. Technicians dressed in white gowns with large rubber gloves and long hollow wands that dispensed a liquid hygienic agent were everywhere. They sprayed the horses from top to bottom with more emphasis on their undercarriages.

Once sprayed, the mare was fitted with a large leather harness. This harness protected her from injury when the stallion mounted.

I watched this scene in quiet fascination. The spraying, the smells, the very loud sounds of the horses, the urgency, the money, you could cut the tension with a sword.

When the stallion mounted his mare, I leaned over to Gaines and whispered loudly in his ear, "He doesn't even buy her a drink?"

Gaines gave me a curious look started to laugh. Others asked him what was so funny. He told them. This large antiseptic, sterile chamber, somber seconds before, erupted in laughter.

## Chapter 14
## United States Capitol

In 1792 Thomas Jefferson proposed a competition for a Capitol Building and residence for the President. Thirty-three year old William Thornton, a physician, painter, inventor and amateur architect won the competition. He had been inspired by the east front of the Louvre and the Pantheon. Since then, many men have served as The Architect of the Capitol. The current dome was designed by Thomas U. Walter and August Schoeborn.

Shortly after completion, the Capitol was partially burned by the British during the War of 1812. Reconstruction was begun immediately and continued until completion in 1864.

The original wooden framed dome was damaged beyond repair, so a new cast iron dome was designed and built. Walter stylized his dome after the dome that Mansart had designed at *Les Invalides*, Paris in 1679.

The installation of Janes, Kirtland and Company's iron castings for the dome was installed by a crew comprised of both black slaves and black freemen. The wood from the original dome was used to fire the steam generated to provide power for the hoisting crane.

Carrère and Hastings designed the new East Front in 1904. Their design brought balance to the dome and the wings of the building.

In 1975 when The Office of the Architect of the Capitol was restoring the Old Senate Chamber they hit a snag because an architectural element could not be produced within the confines of the competitive bidding system.

Late in the day on a hot June evening, Mario Campioli, Assistant Architect of the Capitol, telephoned. I had exited the building, but heard the phone ring and went back to answer it. He introduced himself and said that his office had a seemingly unsolvable problem.

"I'd rather show you than try to explain it on the phone. Can you be in my office tomorrow morning, at nine?"

I thought for a moment and said, "I'll be there."

"Take a taxi from the airport. You won't need a car. I'll have you back in New York for a late lunch."

When I arrived, he and the staff introduced themselves. One member said, "Let's go!"

I fell in stride while the group wound its way to the Old Senate Chamber. A guard let us enter what was essentially a construction site. The famous Old Chamber was having a Renaissance.

I surveyed the site and one thing stood out: the balcony was supported by slender iron pipes, called Lally columns. No one offered an explanation. If a *faux pas* had been committed, talking about it wasn't going to do any good.

I could feel the group mutter, "What do you expect? This is the low bid system at work?"

Campioli said, "We want to have fluted columns with Corinthian capitals." I had learned that all of the Corinthian capitals in the building were different. Each motif represents the indigenous plant of each state. I asked, "Are all of the capitals going to have the same motif?"

"Yes."

They wanted the columns as two longitudinal halves fitted around the Lally columns.

Everyone in the group knew the difficulties inherent in casting these columns in iron. The concave flutes of the pattern would break the sand away when removed from the flask. Preventing this would render the flutes elliptical rather than round. Had the columns been cast in bronze, false cores could have been used to obviate this problem.

This was and is the manner in which all cast iron lampposts were made. The need for visual symmetry was sacrificed for the efficiency of production.

Cast longitudinally, the foundry process would not allow them to remain straight enough to mate and maintain an invisible joint.

I explained that the flutes could be machined to restore the symmetry, but the warp of the castings could not be corrected to ensure a proper mating.

One member of the group was very agitated. In a snappish tone, he said, "Tell us something we don't know."

I was quiet while I pondered this. "Are you familiar with 'drawn over mandrel' tubing?" I asked. "It's the Cadillac of tubular steel. I'm guessing that we can cut it longitudinally without it warping as the stresses are relieved. Then we can machine all of the flutes with similar radii."

Everybody smiled, save for the new nemesis. "What was wrong with this guy?" I thought. But I didn't have time to dwell on it, I marched

*The Old Senate Chamber*
*Photograph courtesy*
*Architect of the Capitol*

onward, "We'll make patterns for the transitional pieces, bases and capitals, cast them in iron and create mechanical and welded connections."

They fell silent. I waited for a verbal snipe from my new "friend." None came.

I was wondering if they had called me here just to get an opinion or if they were going to award this work to us.

They knew that we had been successful with the restoration of Bow Bridge; they were indeed being very ingenious. As we walked back, Campioli said, "Come in my office before you leave, please."

I talked shop with members of the group, then I entered his office to find legal counsel for The Office of the Capitol, Fred Winkleman. Campioli introduced us, saying, "Mr. Fiebiger solved the problem."

Winkleman, said with a slight German accent, "That's a relief." He explained that only *lump sum* contracts were awarded. "For something as special as this we can go around the competitive bidding system, but we need a lump sum price."

We submitted a letter of proposal to which their office

*Benches in the Rotunda*
*Photograph courtesy*
*Architect of the Capitol*

responded via contract, many, many pages of contract. Certified payroll ledgers, reports of union benefits paid and Certificates of Domesticity had to be submitted with requisitions.

The creation of the columns, bases and Corinthian capitals went well. We installed them and received a letter of testimony signed by George M. White.

Yet something was wrong. I called Winklman and said, "I have a problem."

"What?"

"We do all of our work on a time and materials basis. We never make profits like this. It's too much."

The phone went quiet. He wasn't exasperated, just surprised, "Hold on to it. You'll get more work from us. You may still need it."

How prophetic. We lost our proverbial shirts when we made the fences for the East Front of the Capitol.

On display in the lobby of the Office of the Architect of the Capitol was a large wood and glass vitrine that displayed parts of Janes and Kirtland's dome. The dome had been restored during the 1960s.

Displayed were broken flanges of the iron castings and worn out iron bolts. Accompanying the physical elements were photos and highly informative descriptive text. I gave this the title, "Oscillation 101."

Every time I had a meeting with Campioli or Winkleman I studied this vitrine. There were no high strength steel bolts in 1862. The bolts were made of the best iron available at the time, *Genuine Puddled Wrought Iron.*

Wrought iron owes its rust proof properties to its fibrous nature. A.M. Byers Company, Pittsburgh, was a large producer of pipe and bar stock in the U.S. They halted production in mid 1950s. Why? No one knew. The iron work of Venice doesn't rust because it is *Genuine Puddled Wrought Iron.* When it was in the forging processes, waxes--some say beeswax-- were allowed to permeate the open micro texture of the material.

These bolts did not rust, they were worn away by the inexorable motion of the dome. "Oscillation 101" says that as the sun rises every morning, the dome begins to follow its path from east to west through the southern sky. This phenomena takes place with all buildings on the planet.

The dome awakes with the sun and winds itself both clockwise and upward as if reaching for the sun. As the sun moves, some areas retract, other expand. This a body in motion. This knowledge proved invaluable when we began our endeavors for the Statue of Liberty and worked on the Domes of the Main Building of Ellis Island.

A March 15, 2010 letter from Stephen T. Ayers, Acting Architect of the Capitol to me, amplified the forces that are at work.

> "...Your memory about the cast-iron dome oscillating is accurate, although the iron bolts you saw are no longer on display. During the 1959-1960 work on the dome, expansion joints were installed periodically only in the cap rail of the Boilerplate Balcony. The thousands of hairline joints between the iron plates allow for movement during various loading scenarios. Movement in the dome is caused by more than just thermal loading. Gravity forces and wind loads also cause the dome to move. The greatest vertical deformation occurs in the winter, when peak negative thermal loads combined with gravity loads cause a 1-inch downward deflection of the Tholos (i.e., the Capitol is 1 inch shorter on the coldest day in the winter). The greatest normal lateral deflection occurs in the summer under peak unbalanced thermal loads combined with dead loads, which can

*cause a sideward movement of 1.5 inches...."*

When the Office of the Architect of the Capitol had specific commissions that were not highly competitive they called us. Though the jobs were few and far between it was always fun to work with them.

*Old Senate Chamber Franklin Stove*
*Photograph courtesy*
*U.S. Senate Collection*

67

We restored the fences for the Statue of War and The Statue of Peace. We made new fences for the exterior of the East Front, replications of the cast iron benches in the Rotunda, replications of Benjamin Franklin's wood burning stoves and finally, the highly polished bronze stair railings for the entrance to the Senate Chamber.

The railings for the Senate Chamber were unusual because of an invisible joint between the volutes and the handrail molding. This job was difficult because the handrail moldings are extruded bronze in a bronze alloy known as *#385 Architectural Bronze*. The volutes are cast in bronze and there is a slight color difference.

We had the foundry actually smelt the #385 rather than their conventional bronze ingots. We asked them to gamble. They poured different measured amounts of aluminum powder to alter the color. We hit a home run on the first pitch; the colors matched.

Opa had taught us this "trick." We even showed it on shop drawings, but nobody believed us until they saw railings.

Opa's second trick was to join the two pieces by *upsetting* each of the mating edges. Each edge was hammered upwards to be larger than it is. Aligned holes were drilled in the mating parts; stainless steel dowels were friction fitted. The two pieces were forced together and were welded on the bottom only. The *upset* joints looked ugly for a while, but then they were aligned. The weld was then cleaned and polished making the joint invisible.

Belts and suspenders once again. Held firmly in place now, the raised joints were hammered down. When they appeared to be a little above the desired destination, the hammering stopped and the filing and polishing began.

## Chapter 16
## Morgan Library & Museum, New York City

John Pierpont Morgan, JP, was always a lucky man! Morgan and his three hundred and fifty one containers of art that he collected in Europe were scheduled to travel on the maiden voyage of the RMS *Titanic*. He cancelled at the last minute.

Once his empire was established, he collected rare books and art. He hired fifty-two year old Charles F. McKim in 1902 to be the architect for all phases of the exterior and interior design of his library.

McKim, a principal in the firm of McKim, Mead and White, was the acknowledged master of the "American Renaissance.".All of the principals in the firm had attended the *École des Beaux-Arts*. The *École's* classical Greek and Roman style dominated their commissions.

Morgan collected *incunabula* (books *print*ed before 1501), prints, sculpture and drawings of great European artists. In 1924 his son Jack made

*Entrance gates & side lites*

the library a public institution to honor his father.

We performed restorative and new commissions at the Morgan for over twenty-five years. We restored the iron fences and gates of Morgan's residence, restored the bronze fences and gates to the Library that is adjacent to the residence, repaired the bronze entrance doors, restored a bronze statue of *Running Eros* from the first ruins of Pompeii (AD 79), executed the ironwork for the handicap access ramp, and made bronze windows, stair railings, window grilles, and vitrines to house the collection of Michelangelo's sketches. What great fun we had. How lucky we were.

We began the restoration of the iron fences and gates by having samples of paint surgically removed, like skin lesions, from the surface. The paint chips were studied under a spectrum microscope that determined the numbers of layers of paint and the amount of dirt and grit that began to corrode the work. The corrosion followed New York City's time line and was consistent with construction of the Midtown Tunnel and its traffic flowing past the library. Fascinating! A hundred years of New York City history found in a quarter-inch-thick slice of paint.

Dr. Charles Ryskamp was the Director of the Morgan. Tall, handsome and proletarian, he was soaked with charm, graciousness, knowledge and talent. I always felt privileged when in his presence. After we completed the restoration of the approximately two hundred and fifty feet of fence, and entrance gates with side lights and bronze bulletin board he sent this handwritten note:

> *"15 March, 1970*
> *The Ides of March*
> *Dear Joe,*
>
> *These are my personal gifts to*
> *you and your men on the occasion of your*

*completion of the fences. You have done a*
*marvellous job and this is just a small way of*
*saying thank you*

*The champagne comes with*
*my heartfelt gratitude.*

*Yours sincerely,*
*Charles Ryskamp"*

There were two bottles of champagne. We opened one of them around the large layout bench on the main floor of the shop. I gave copies of the note to each of the men and we toasted him.

We opened the second bottle ten months later to toast the birth of my son Paul.

A few years later, when restoring the bronze gates and fences we commissioned, the Metropolitan Museum's preservationist, Steven Weintraub to study and report on the history of the bronze. The bronze showed much dirt and grime, but no traces of corrosion

Ten years later we also found this to be true with the Statue of Liberty. The assumed loss of material on each was one micron (an average strand of human hair is approximately eighty-eight microns).

Are you wondering why these bronze masterpieces were in need of restoration? Everybody else was. The facts were irrefutable, the fences and gates were falling apart, yet there was no evidence of corrosion.

The mystery was revealed when we removed the first screw. All of the screws were iron. They had been brass plated in order to patinate in concert with the bronze. Electromotive forces were at work. The iron was spent. Their deterioration allowed the bronze elements to separate. The only thing holding the elements together was habit. Minor damage to the bronze was only cosmetic.

This was a major commission. Why had the foundry done this?

Why did they take a such a shortcut? Money? Unavailability of material? Did they think that plating was sufficient interface to obviate this galvanic process? Did they know about the galvanic process? The answer to this is, emphatically, yes. Was it nefarious? We will never know.

The mechanical fasteners problem was exacerbated when their size was determined. The screws that held the elements were flat head machine screws of an unusual size. The fences for the Library were cast in bronze as faithful reproductions of their older iron models. The iron fences we knew were fastened with conventional one quarter inch diameter screws with twenty threads per inch.

The bronze fences were held with seventeen sixty-fourths (one sixty-fourth of an inch larger than one quarter of an inch). Before the Society of American Engineers was born in 1905 there were no standardized sizes. Shops made whatever sizes suited them.

The responsibility of an artisan in a restoration project is to restore the original state, leaving as little evidence of the restoration as possible. We had a few choices, none of them within the defined parameters. Closing all of the holes by welding and then drilling and taping new holes for one quarter inch diameter screws was out of the question. We could open the existing holes for five sixteenths of an inch diameter screws, but the diameter of the heads was too large.

We had 5,000 brass screws manufactured by Industrial Fasteners Corporation to conform to the original screw size. The new screws were faithful in replication. The heads were the same and were noted by their invisibility. The restoration was pure. Though all the elements were disassembled, the original patina was never abraded. The only chemically applied patinas were to the screw heads.

The great philanthropist and devotee of the Metropolitan Opera, Betty Wold Johnson was also a great friend to the Morgan Library. She funded this restoration and took great interest in it. Once completed, she,

*Bronze entrance gates & side lites*

Ryskamp and I celebrated. We met on the lawn on a warm spring evening in Manhattan with evening rush hour traffic crawling towards the Midtown Tunnel. Always charming, Ryskamp, presided in an informal manner. Johnson wore a flowered spring dress with a shawl. A white gloved attendant served a magnum of champagne from a silver tray with stemmed plastic glasses. A light zephyr had come up, it coaxed traffic fumes away. It ruffled the ever fastidious Ryskamp's hair and Johnson's gossamery scarf. No one complained. We ate caviar, drank champagne and toasted the largess of Johnson while she toasted our efforts. Ryskamp, ever gracious, thanked us both. The fences and gates looked, we all imagined, as they did when McKim had originally commissioned them.

Taken with the event, Johnson invited Ryskamp and me, with my family, to her New Jersey farm to once again celebrate the completion of the project.

Balinda and I explained to our nine-year-old daughter, Beth, and three-year old son, Paul, that Johnson, through her company, had invented the Band-Aid. They certainly knew about Band-Aids.

It was another wonderful spring day. After lunch, Johnson asked Balinda if she and the children would like to see her gardens. Mr. Johnson, Ryskamp and I lingered a while and then joined the gardeners.

Balinda and the kids helped Johnson tend to the garden, albeit gingerly. Perhaps not gingerly enough, for Paul cut his finger. Nothing too severe, but bleeding.

Balinda put a tissue over the wound and kissed it. Johnson went inside to look for a Band-Aid. She returned to report that as they were still settling in to the new house, and they had no Band-Aids. Was it okay to laugh? Wry smiles served well.

Three-year old Paul, understood everything and yet it did not register. The look on his face was not fear or pain but bewilderment. Balinda reached into her purse and plucked out a ratty, crumpled, sealed, Curad. She held it in her fingers, looked to Johnson rather sheepishly. Johnson smiled and said, "Of course, dear."

Smiles and laughter were okay.

A few years later I accompanied Johnson and her friends on a boat tour to the Statue of Liberty. When Johnson and I met again, with a twinkle in her eye, she asked, "How's your son's finger?"

I had enlisted the aid of Ryskamp in fund raising for Statue of Liberty/ Ellis Island Foundation. I gave a lecture on the restoration in progress and a historical narrative.

The Statue of Liberty/Ellis Island Foundation provided a small craft, box lunches with hors d'oeuvres, wine and champagne. Unfortunately, the March weather was foul. We did have plastic glasses, but certainly no silver trays. All in attendance were "good sports." They enjoyed the lecture, were gracious with their contributions and were glad to disembark to warmer environs.

In 1979 Ryskamp and his staff presented an exhibition entitled *Michelangelo and His World*. They had acquired sketches, notes and line drawings of Michelangelo.

Ryskamp called upon us to assist in the design of the forged iron and walnut displays to show these works. There were to be vertical displays with forged iron legs and bases attached to polished walnut ledges and horizontal vitrines to encapsulate the art, nice, but pleasingly nondescript.

It was the treat of a lifetime, making something that touched the work of the great Michelangelo.

Ryskamp wrote on April 26, 1979,

> *"Dear Joe,*
>
> *I want to thank you for all that you did to make our exhibition of Michelangelo and His World a success. It truly is a great accomplishment. I may be prejudiced, but I do believe that it is as fine an installation, with as excellent design and workmanship in all ways, as I have ever seen. Without your help—your devotion—it would not have been possible.*
>
> *I hope you will give my heartfelt thanks to everyone who worked with you for this exhibition.*
>
> *Sincerely yours,*
> *Charles Ryskamp, Director"*

Morgan hired Belle da Costa Greene in 1905. Greene, a light skinned Negress, passed as Portuguese to explain the brown tinge of her complexion. A woman of exceptional talent, Morgan cared not that she was African-

American. What counted were her talents. It led her across boundaries of America's color line and provided an extraordinary life.

Because he found her vivacious, brilliant and cunning, Morgan gave her *carte blanche* to acquire the treasures of art that comprised his private collection. She traveled to Europe constantly and dealt with the art world's most powerful men, some of whom she took as lovers. Noteworthy is that Morgan and she were never reported to have entered that liaison.

Greene was known as "the soul of the Morgan Library." She retired from the Library in 1948 and died in 1950 at the age of seventy.

One of Greene's great acquisitions was a eight-inch-tall bronze statue of *Running Eros*. Supposed to have been one of Morgan's favorites, the statue had been excavated from the ruins of Roman villas located in Boscoreale, Italy. The statue was buried in the same eruption of Mt. Vesuvius that destroyed in Pompeii in AD 79.

We soon learned that *Running Eros* (Cupid) had a personality, a pulse, a smile. But the wings had fallen off. Ryskamp called and asked if we could be enlisted to perform the surgical reattachment. Paramount was that the reattachment be performed while leaving no traces of the restoration.

This patina was like none other. It was not just the evolution of colors through the time line of copper, it was a product of the hot lava and time. It had the verdigris color of aged copper and deposits of lava that had been atomically bonded. The deposits were porous, irregularly

*Running Eros*

shaped and had varying thinness. Conservators and preservationists with whom I had discussed this, were happily surprised that the heat of the lava had not eviscerated the statue.

Application of any heat would damage the patina. Drilling new holes would violate the integrity of the art. Introduction of a new metal, i.e. lead, for ballast, was unacceptable. How then to make this reconnection? It couldn't be welded, brazed or soldered. New holes couldn't be drilled to make mechanical connections.

This is why I always slept with a pad and pencil by the night stand. Lying in bed, playing this out, the solution presented itself. There were holes in the body of the statue where the wings had originally been connected. Since there were no threaded connections in AD 79, the wings had been attached via bronze dowels with a friction fit. This was most likely the cause of the failure. There were some other holes that had either been used to vent the gasses during the lost wax casting process or were a function of the burning lava.

First things first: we measured, cleaned and defrosted the lunch room freezer. It was a combination refrigerator/freezer. The refrigerator was used for lunches, condiments, sodas and welding rods. The freezer was unused, save for ice cubes. Now it had a task to perform. It would be the test chamber for our experiment.

Could we attach the wings with bronze wire, pass the wire through the original holes and find a material viscous enough to pour, yet be inert and hold the wires firmly? The first step was to attach the wings to the body with the bronze wire. Then we poured distilled water into the eight inch tall statue and put him in the freezer.

The next morning, frozen like a rock, the wings were firmly in place. Now the hunt was on. No lead, no ice, what then? I called Richard Knoor of Techno-Craft. Knoor made patterns for castings, we had worked together on many projects, one of them being the female impression for the new, repoussé copper nose for the Statue of Liberty.

I asked Knoor if any of the polymers and urethanes that he used to make the patterns were inert and viscous enough to pour though the existing three eighths of an inch diameter hole that we used to pour the water. He said yes.

Now the big question: With the small amount of space inside the body, would the polymer be enough to hold the wires? Again, Knoor said yes.

Ranieri hammered a copper form to represent the corpus of the statue and made a pair of rudimentary wings. We welded a bottom to it and essentially created a crude form of *Running Eros*.

We attached the bronze wires to the wings, passed them through the holes and waited for Knoor to mix his materials. Ranieri held the wings in place, Knoor poured his late 20th century brew through a long-stemmed funnel and we held our collective breaths. It worked!

The next problem: *Running Eros* was a closed vessel. We knew that we had a procedure that complied with most of requirements for a late 20th century restoration, except for one. It was not reversible.

Ryskamp was involved with all of the facets of the restoration. He was the only one who could make this decision. He had a few choices: leave the wings unattached, and abort the attempt at restoration; proceed with the restoration based upon our studies and ignore, albeit grudgingly, the non-reversible feature; or he could find smarter people.

We found a very minor compromise. We could not reverse the polymer, but we could leave a small amount of bronze wire, tightly wound and unnoticeable at the interface of the wings and body. If the wings ever had to be removed, they could be unattached. Enough surplus wire would be in place to aid the new restorer.

Ryskamp chose to employ this compromise and the restoration was successfully completed. We all stood around the carpeted workbench and admired the restored *Eros*. The late afternoon sun-yes you can see it in Manhattan-shone in the style of Tintoretto, through the windows and cast its key light on *Running Eros*. It was mesmerizing.

Usually one doesn't notice the smell in an atelier such as ours; it's just taken for granted. Now it was dominant. At that point in time, if pride had a smell, this was it. Ranieri said, "He looks happy." Then, as he always said when a commission was ended, "Another job done!"

He didn't have to ask what the next one was, he already knew. All the men knew. An important part of company policy was that the men knew their jobs were secure.

Now the issue was delivery. How to get him home? We had all worn gloves during the restoration. Perspiration had not touched him, nor packing materials, only cheesecloth. Ranieri suggested that he and I deliver it to the Morgan the next day. He would place cheesecloth in his hands and on his lap. I would drive while he held it.

*Running Eros* was literally priceless. At the end of the work day he was wrapped gently in cheesecloth and placed in our office safe. This safe was not too safe. It had been burgled twice and still had the fingerprint powder all over it from the last police procedure. Nonetheless, there he was placed. All this had been discussed with Ryskamp. *Running Eros* was insured with their fine arts coverage. Yogi Berra might have said that it was "Worth so much that it was worthless."

No commission had ever been more challenging. How we all enjoyed it! Sounds crazy, I know, but I think that *Eros* appreciated having his wings reattached.

# Chapter 17
## The Frick Collection, New York

Henry Clay Frick vowed to be a millionaire by the age of thirty. He was. His fortune secured, he developed his love for art. He commissioned the architectural firm of Carrère and Hastings to design his mansion at Seventieth Street and Fifth Avenue.

Construction of another of the firm's masterpieces began in 1913. Carrère, fifty-three, was killed in an automobile accident in 1911. Frick's intention, to bequeath his mansion and art collection to the public required specific architectural features. Hastings and his staff did them well. A visit to the atrium of The Collection was considered to be an amazing event. Beauty and serenity were unparalleled in the heart of New York City.

In 1977 a garden was added east of The Collection on East Seventieth Street. British landscape architect and garden designer Russell Page was commissioned to design it.

The new Reception Hall to accommodate the garden was designed by architects John Barrington Bailey, Harry van Dyke and G. Frederick Poehler. Bailey, along with Henry Hope Reed and Pierce Rice had cofounded Classical America in 1968. It became The Institute of Classical Architecture and Classical America in 2002.

Paramount to the success of these works was the need to precisely replicate the decorative iron fences and piers. The Collection had maintained a large set of entrance gates that they wanted to restore and incorporate into the assembly. The iron fences and piers were to be mounted atop limestone retaining walls.

We were awarded the commission. The work was to be performed on a time and materials basis with a guaranteed maximum sum. Labor was charged at prevailing rates with an allowance for changes to the collective bargaining agreement with the union. Materials other than iron were charged at cost, plus fifteen percent for profit. We maintained an old world custom of never charging for iron. It engendered the spirit of good will between patron and artisan. These commissions were labor intensive, iron was still usually one percent of the total cost. We furnished labor schedules and material schedules with copies of invoices from suppliers. Certificates of receipt of payments and Certificates of Domesticity for materials were also furnished. Our letter of proposal defined our strong belief in the responsibility we had to the art that we served. And we meant it!

Fortunately, The Frick had a small section of unused fence and one decorative pier (column). As Opa had done when replicating iron grilles for Mr. Rockefeller, we disassembled these pieces in order to replicate the elements. The length of ninety-nine feet, eleven and five eighths inches was divided disproportionately. The entrance gates were, appropriately, on the center line of the garden but not the center line of fence. There were five plinths that interrupt the limestone wall in order to please the eye. Atop these plinths rested the intricate forged and repoussé piers. The most notable

Forged fences and piers

81

element of the pier, as described by David Monroe Collins, financial officer of The Frick, "was a very proud eagle." The lengths between these piers were all different.

This was the first of many challenges to overcome. The basic motif of the fence called for two styles of pickets: a large, or major picket twelve inches tall; and a minor picket six inches tall. Each fence had to end with a major picket. This dilemma had not been solved by those who made the fences on Fifth Avenue, fence sections ended at piers with no balance for the odd-even format. How to solve this arithmetic puzzle? How to solve it without the aid of a computer? But solve it we did. We expanded or shrunk the center positioning of the seven-eights of an inch square vertical bars by mere thousandths of an inch and maintained the visual discipline required. It was almost one hundred feet long and tolerances of one thirty-second of an inch. Great in theory, but how to maintain it?

We had planned to punch holes in the horizontal members through which to pass those vertical bars. We had a machine with more than enough tonnage to perform this task. But its percussive force stretched the iron;

Entrance portal to the gardens

*arithmetic crawl* would defeat our quest for precision. It was mandatory that the length of each fence be maintained.

There were alternative ways to accomplish this. We settled on making drill jigs with drill bushings and drilling little round holes to comprise the square. The rough holes were filed by hand. The dimensional integrity of the fences was maintained! Repetitive and boring tasks, the men took turns filing the 800 holes.

Every day the smiths worked forging the hundreds of scrolls. The scrolls had to be forged to a taper before the terminal buttons could be forged. Then they had to be formed while hot to fit the jigs that created their form.

Members of The Collection and the architects would visit the shop to inspect the work on a regular basis. This was always a pleasant experience. I used to kid them, that I thought that they really came just to enjoy the Bill of Fare and Martinis at the famous Empire Diner at Tenth Avenue and 22nd Street.

Each of the seven-eighths inch square vertical bars had a decorative tassel on it. The original fences had been made in a fashion of eras past, when the smith could have an iron foundry cast an iron element directly onto the bar. That procedure was unavailable to us. We had two choices, we could have the tassels cast in iron with a square hole in the center and then rivet it in place or we could cast it on, with lead. Slipping an iron casting over the bar was to our way of thinking, "sloppy." The joint would be hard to hide and it could allow water entry. We opted for virgin lead.

A four-sided die with the negative impression of the tassel was made. Each bar was deformed to hold the lead. The bar was taken to cherry red heat (1400 F.), placed in a jig that held the four-sided die. Using ladles, the molten lead (630 F.) was poured into the die. Allowed to cool, the die was separated, the lead was cleaned and chased with chisels.

Collins had asked that we explore the expanding technology of applied coatings. Conventional red lead had been discovered to be carcinogenic if ingested. Obviously no one was going to eat the paint from a fence. But all the same, its disfavor was driving it off the market. Manufacturers would make special batch orders but there were other arcane features. The most notable were the number of mils (one mil = one thousandth of an inch, one strand of human is four mils) required to provide rust inhibition. Optimum paint thickness required with Linseed Oil-based red lead was eight mils for the primer and four mils for the finish coat. Such thickness dulls the sharp details of fine work.

We called various experts in the materials coating field. Highly recommended was the Tnemec Company and their relatively new line of organic and inorganic zinc finishing systems. Tnemec had a system of *cathodic retardation*. Simply put, zinc being less noble than iron, sacrifices itself to protect the more noble family member, iron.

The system required a micro-blasted texture. This clean yet mildly abraded texture allows the zinc and its proprietary binding agent to fill the microscopic peaks and valleys and effect a mechanical bond.

The silica content made blasting with sand a health hazard. Many products with no deleterious side effects had entered the arena to achieve various degrees of porosity and hardness. Walnut shells, corn cobs, glass beads, metal shot and other non silica products were notable replacements. We chose a system to work in concert with our compressed air supply equipment. A balance of feet per second of air and air pressure had to be set in balance with diameter of the blasting nozzle. This proper balance enabled the operator to remove as little metal as possible while creating the peaks and valleys.

We made large painting easels that rotated like barbecue spits. The fences, gates or piers were mounted on the easels, they were rolled into the micro-blasting chamber, the pressure pot was filled, and air settings were established. The operator donned a hood fed with filtered air and the process began. A large downdraft dust collection system kept the chamber's environment clean but noisy.

The organic zinc coating was applied as soon as the work pieces were rolled from the chamber. The gray, raw finish of the work piece was never touched with an ungloved hand. Zinc was placed in a pressurized pot with an impeller. Zinc and Tnemec's proprietary binder were mixed, and the impeller kept them in a suspended state.

Optimum rust inhibition would be obtained with two mils of zinc followed by two mils of a proprietary sealer and then with two mils of the final black coat. Mil readings were taken after each phase.

We made drill templates to precisely locate the holes in the limestone walls. These were to encapsulate the structural members of the fences and piers. We owned sophisticated diamond drilling equipment. Diamond drills allowed three-inch diameter holes to be drilled through the limestone caps into the reinforced concrete walls. They cut through a stainless steel flashing member easily. Diamond drills, however, must be cooled with water as they drill.

In 1916, the New York City Building Department devised a unique formula that related to the width of the street and the heights of the buildings. It mandated that *setbacks* be used as the buildings ascended. This attempted to assure that light and fresh air would reach the streets. I think that this only works on East Seventieth Street for the summer and winter equinoxes.

I was pleased when lifetime friend Patrick Martucci came to work with us. He had been an automobile mechanic for the greater part of his life and chose us as an alternative career.

On a cold February day he laid out the drilling templates that established the exact positions for the holes. He set up the drilling equipment and connected the fresh water supply.

We had a major problem, we could not be sure that we could get all of the water out of the holes after drilling. We could blow them out with compressed air, even vacuum them out with a vacuum pump, but we could not dry out the limestone. Via capillary action a residue would leach to the bottom of the holes and freeze. Would the resulting ice crack the limestone? We didn't want to find out.

Martucci and I were talking about our possible choices. We could pour small amounts of automotive antifreeze into the holes. It would prevent the freezing and breaking. Unfortunately it could discolor the limestone if it leached through. Unacceptable! Would tightly packed straw produce enough of a thermal barrier to prevent freezing? Too many unknowns.

As he and I were talking, a group of businessmen and women, dressed in colored scarfs and heavy overcoats, walked by. When they left, in their wake was a smell of something familiar.

"Do you smell that?" I asked.

"Gin," he said.

Our eyes met, we smiled, we laughed.

"I'll go buy some gin. The holes will never freeze."

"Buy vodka," he said, "It won't smell."

Vodka certainly had the ability to prevent freezing. It would not discolor and it did not smell. I bought three bottles of cheap vodka and Martucci poured it in the holes after he drilled them. The next morning there was no ice, no stain and little vodka. Necessity is surely the mother of invention.

Installation of the fences, piers and gates went splendidly. We had maintained our one thirty second of an inch tolerance. Each two-ton gate leaf opened with the ease of pushing a baby carriage. This was as close to perfect as possible.

We had an ad hoc meeting on the sidewalk in front of the fences one morning with a few trustees, Collins and myself. Collins said, "Congratulations, it's an amazing piece of work." Rather sheepishly he continued, "I don't want to hurt your feelings, Joe, but they look like plastic. When you have moment, come up to my office."

In the office he said, "I didn't want to hurt your feelings about the paint. Coffee?"

"Thanks"

"I'm disappointed with it, too. Their swatches didn't show the gloss to be so prominent. Was it worth the trade, the thin coverage and no loss of detail?"

"I guess we'll just have to wait and see."

Others had entered his office and someone said, "New York traffic will take that gloss away pretty fast."

"I hope so," Collins said.

His eyes twinkled mischievously. "Want to hear a funny story?"

We all nodded.

"Miss Frick went on a short holiday. She left the staff in charge, as she usually did. Anyway, the phone company called, talked with an upstairs maid and offered to exchange the old black dial phones for new *touch tone* Princesses."

He smiled and took a sip of coffee. "They exchanged the phones. When Miss Frick found out she was furious. She wanted her old phones back. The poor maid was in tears for days. She kept her job because Miss Frick felt so sorry for her."

"Miss Frick's lawyer called the phone company and asked for the phones back. He was told that it was too late, they were gone to the 'Ye Olde Motel' in Vermont.'"

Collins grinned, "The lawyer told the phone company executive to 'just get the damn things back.'"

"No," he was told. Now the attorney was angry. He said, "I can suggest two choices to Miss Frick. She can buy the motel or she can sell all of her phone company stock. 'I think I'll tell her to sell the stock.'"

Collins laughed. "The phone went silent for a moment and the phone executive said, 'The phones will be back in place in a few days.' They were, too."

Everyone in the room enjoyed the tale. I thanked Collins and exited with a sad heart. A commission with over 13,500 hours of labor, no corners cut, no shortcuts, a labor of love for many talented artisans fell to the mercy of rust-inhibiting, glossy paint. Ironic! Use the proven system and apply so much paint that the details are dulled or try something new that will not hide the details and yet fail.

Was there a remedy other than the hopeful application of a New York City air patina? Time passed and the plastic sheen dulled.

Six years later a catastrophe! The entire system began to fail. Lumps of paint, all three coats, some the size of potato chips peeled off and fell to the ground. What was happening? There was a electrolytic failure in progress.

The Tnemec Company was called in. They did guarantee their product, but only for the cost of materials. Though the cost of materials was appreciable-it paled compared to the costs of labor in a controlled interior environment. This pleased no one. Neither did Tnemec's evaluation of the possible causes of the failure which were: operator had mayonnaise on his hands while applying paint; or an act of God.

Collins asked me in an incredulous tone, "Did they really say that? They blamed God? Did they think that lightning struck it?"

I had no appropriate answer. I was the messenger.

He was quiet for a moment and asked me to find the cause and a remedy. He was adamant that I was not to be blamed for this failure. He said that sometimes these things happened when the envelope was pushed. He was strong on this point and believed that there were times it still had to be pushed.

During lunch at The Collection a group of us speculated. Was this a variation of *regression toward the mean*? Something so close to perfection rendered imperfect from an alien source? We decided to re-read the fifth chapter of the my imaginary book, *Go Figure*.

Time for the cavalry. Enter our resident genius and good friend, Richard Smith. A noted scientist and metallurgist, Smith began measuring the electromotive forces by taking Pico amperage readings. He acknowledged that the zinc electrons and protons were indeed spending themselves. But, he didn't know why. What was in this poly-metallic mix that would send a false signal? We identified all the known dissimilar metals that we had used: lead; bronze; and copper. Smith was certain that these were not the culprits.

When the reinforced concrete walls had been poured, electrical conduits had been placed for garden lights. The concrete walls were flashed with stainless steel. Smith mused that there was a mild electromotive short circuit between the galvanized (zinc) conduit and the stainless steel. This situation was deemed a "phenomena." Smith's remedy-break the connection by encapsulating the iron work in a nonmetallic envelope.

The Collection was appreciative of our efforts and had us refinish the fences, piers and gates according to Smith's advice. Smith's parting opinion was "Sometimes you can't explain, you just have to accept it and live to fight another day."

Page Cross told me that Henry Hope Reed said to him over lunch, "The new fences and piers at The Frick may be the best ironwork in New York City in the late 20th century." Cross responded, "We'll just have to wait and see."

So paradoxical that a love story between artisans and the work that they created was tainted by something so alien.

Soon after he became Director of the Frick Collection, Charles Ryskamp asked me to visit him. He wanted a five year plan in effect for the restoration of the original fences and piers.

I explained that I had kept a vigilante "eye" and note book on them, since the 1977 request of Collins. The fence had been "leaning" inward. I simply kept a log as the out-of-plumb condition worsened.

He obviously remembered the iron screws that held the bronze fences together at the Morgan Library. "Is there anything crucial going on? Are we in an emergency situation? What's holding them up?"

"The braces are holding them. Don't worry, they won't just go 'Bong!' and bounce across the street." He smiled, nodded and walked to a bookcase.

He gave me a recently published book of the works of art at the Frick. He knew that Balinda was a bibliophile and said, "Your wife will like this. The publisher forgot to number the pages. I know that you're still tied up with Ellis Island, but put a three phase plan together for me. Can you stretch it over five years?"

"Of course."

"Do you still have a moment?

I nodded and smiled.

"What have you learned on your odyssey with Lady Liberty?"

"Wow! That's a loaded question. I wish I had studied more sociology. We needed Margaret Meade out there, maybe Sigmund Freud, too. Greed and ego. I never saw greed before. People behaved differently at the end than at the beginning."

"Joe, you told me how you took the impressions for the nose. Could we apply that technique to take impressions of the bas relief on our limestone columns? I would like to save the details before they're worn away. Its a well kept secret, but many of the great sculptural pieces have their details saved."

"Dr. Ryskamp," I said. "I certainly can have Hoheb and his daughter take the impressions. If you ever need to enhance the details the carvers will have accurate models. There's another way, very up and coming technology."

"I was hoping that you'd tell me about something like this."

"Photogrammerty. Its digital photography to a millionth of an inch. It's just emerging from infancy."

"How does one use it?"

"Computerized machinery is expanding exponentially. A 'Five Axis Machine' is being developed. I don't understand the name, There is an X, Y, Z and an angular axis," I said as I held my fingers at a forty-five degree angle. "That's only four, I don't know what the fifth is."

"It handshakes with the data generated from the photogrammetric camera and like a milling machine, carves that data into any metal or wax."

"How did hear about this?"

"Greed and ego, yes, but lots of smart people out there. I just listened."

He asked, "What kind of a chap is Mr. Iacocca?"

"I've only met him a few times. When he's on the island he has a big following. It's a team meeting and he's the coach, well, maybe the owner. He fields all questions and is very witty. I've been at the back of the group a few times and listened. He knows everything. Apparently the auto and movie industries are developing these new technologies."

He stood up and said, "Thanks for enlightening me. When we finish the second phase, if you're ahead of your budget, maybe we'll take the impressions."

# Chapter 18
## Metropolitan Museum of Art, New York

"What do you know about stairs?" Steven Weintraub, Conservator and Preservationist at the Metropolitan Museum of Art called to ask.

"Not enough. Can't ever know enough."

He scratched the surface about a dilemma of sorts. "Can you meet me tomorrow? Ten o'clock?"

"Sure."

"Go to the information desk, they'll call me and I'll come and get you."

"Are you going to have a flower in your lapel?" I asked.

I heard him smile, "I'll find you."

As I drove to the Met on a warm October day in 1978 I wondered what lay ahead. Working for the Met was every artisan's dream. I did what I always did when I was nervous, I licked the tips of the fingers of my right hand. It always brought the butterflies back to normal.

A receptionist at the information desk called him to announce my arrival. A minute or so later found me. He was in his early thirties, of medium build and handsome, with a professorial look.

I asked, "Will you guide me out of here?"

"No"

He searched his pockets and pretended to hand something to me. His eyes were aglow, he laughed and said, "Start dropping the crumbs, you'll find your way out."

I liked this guy already. A lifetime friendship was born that day.

On our way out of the Great Hall we passed the flowers that are the daily gift of Lila Acheson Wallace. He saw that I had looked at the plaque and said, "She helped finance the bridge you did in Central Park, didn't she?"

"Yes, she's a really nice lady."

He asked, "Do you know any of the history of this place? We're walking through the first version that your boys from Central Park made."

"Who?"

"Mould and Vaux designed it in the early 1870s. Everybody hated it, they called it a 'mausoleum.' It got gobbled up when they hired Hunt to be the architect for the Great Hall. He died in 1895 and McKim, Meade and White came along. They added the wings. All Beaux Arts architecture."

"How involved was Morgan?" I asked.

"John Jay started it. He wanted to build a museum that wouldn't be in the control of one guy. He put a group of business men, politicos and artists together and made it happen. Morgan was one of them."

We had walked a long time and I was running out of crumbs. He read my mind, "We're almost there. The building is a quarter of a mile long, more than two million square feet."

We entered the construction site that was the American Wing. Kevin Roche and John Dinkeloo, Roche and Dinkeloo, Architects, were melding the building and the park.

The interior of the building was comprised of a large courtyard at ground level and a second floor mezzanine. An architectural attachment was needed. The architects had decided to use two scissor type staircases to provide easy passage between the levels. The Chicago Stock Exchange Building was being razed and Louis Sullivan's masterpiece staircase was available. Could it be made to fit was the question?

Richard Nickel was a proponent of saving elements of Sullivan's works. He had served as an archivist for the Metropolitan Museum during the demolition of the Chicago Stock Exchange Building in the early 1970s. Unfortunately, the floor above collapsed and killed him.

Louis Henri Sullivan was born in Massachusetts. In 1872 he attended the Massachusetts Institute of Technology at the age of sixteen. He left after one year and landed a position in Philadelphia with architect, Frank Furness. The depression of 1873 forced Furness to discharge Sullivan. Sullivan moved to the Windy City to be a part of the Chicago's recovery from the 1875 Great Fire.

Dankmar Adler, twelve years senior, hired Sullivan in 1879. His mother died giving him birth. His father expressed his sadness and thanks with the name Dankmar. It is combination: *Dank* for thanks, *mar* for bitter, "bitter thanks." Adler was a pioneer and leader in developing and building steel-framed skyscrapers in the 1880s. He was also a pioneer in acoustics.

A year later Sullivan became a partner in the firm. They hired the young Frank Lloyd Wright. Wright became a disciple of Sullivan.

Sullivan's talents were recognized and he was soon called "father of the American skyscraper." He was the first to defy the limits of weight-bearing masonry and defined new limits by using structural steel for power and grace. He introduced a new vocabulary: "high rise, base, shaft, pediment, load bearing, etc." Though used by many who followed him, he is supposed to have coined the phrase "form follows function."

Revered by many, his works carry his signature of ornament, grace and power.

The museum staff had carefully laid all of the elements. But in the lexicon of the day, they did not know the "guzentas (goes into) from the "goezoutas" (goes out of). A mess! But not for long. The logic, the mechanics of the assembly presented themselves very quickly. A few days later I took Master Craftsman, Gennaro Ranieri with me to study these shapes and to meet museum staff. Ranieri, when he came to work with us in 1967, picked up the nickname Bruno because he was strong, and handsome like the famous wrestler of the era, Bruno Sanmartino.

Ranieri was born in 1931 and raised in the Abruzzi Mountains of Italy. He was born to work metals. His wisdom was deep and talents were many. We spoke many languages in our shop, but the universal language was good work. Ranieri and I could read each other's minds. Talk from A to B to C and by C, he was already to M. We worked together like this for twenty-eight years.

We looked at each other and smiled. He said, "Do we have this job yet?"

"Not yet."

"I hope we get it. It'll be fun."

We both knew where every piece was supposed to go. It was indeed a masterpiece of art and architecture, but it was also a masterpiece of logic. It would be one of the only elements in the museum that was both an accessioned art object, given a number in the museum's system, and a piece of architecture.

As we grew to know the stair, we grew to know Sullivan and his noted foundry, Winslow Brothers. In our company library we had a 1910 edition of their catalog. It held the body of who they were, what they did, and for us, how they did it. We believed that Sullivan sat with Winslow's draftsmen and engineers, sketched the motifs for the stringers, risers, balustrades, facias, etc. and then passed the design baton on to them.

Winslow Brothers was a large facility with multiple facets of work, a foundry for both iron and bronze, pattern makers, wood carvers, electroplaters, and blacksmiths.

A cute technique that Winslow had was to turn iron into copper. They cast in iron and electroplated the iron with copper. The copper was then patinated.

The death of Nickel had left the project in chaos. Disassembled, the stair parts were allowed to sit out of doors, unprotected, through a Chicago winter. The iron and copper interface was violated.

Our Tenth Avenue shop consisted of two buildings and a rear yard. Though the ceiling in the main shop was twelve feet high, it would not accommodate the erection of the stair and its connections to the landings.

Lewis Sharp, assistant director of the American Wing, was active in all phases of the restoration. He had a talent to designate the right people, at the right time, for the right job. He trusted them and was rewarded for that trust.

He and staff members, Maurice Heckscher, James Pilgrim, Ann Winston, Henry Wolcott, Craig Miller and Steven Weintraub visited our shop, en mass. We put more water in the coffee, bought more donuts and had an ad hoc meeting. They rolled up their sleeves, got dirty, touched some of the pieces in the prototype, and watched them being trial assembled, and talked with the men. They wanted to know us as artisans, craftsmen and people. We discussed the basics of layout and materials handling. We were still far away from the restoration process. We could not erect the stair in our open rear yard because we would be inviting more corrosion. We agreed to build a temporary structure to enclose the rear yard. The museum agreed to share a portion of this cost.

Once again we were in new waters. I made schedules of labor and materials of all of the phases of work that I could identify. The trick here was not to estimate the labor and materials precisely, but to identify all of functions required. I presented our proposal based on our usual cost plus, time and materials procedure.

Our proposal was reviewed by business officers of the museum. I was called to a meeting to discuss the proposal. Sharp escorted me to a meeting with the museum's construction manager, Arthur Klien. Always dignified, always the ambassador, with the look of somewhat rumpled college professor, Sharp held my left elbow and led me to Klien's office. I kept hearing my father telling me, "If you have to sell it, it shouldn't be bought."

Sharp introduced me to Klien, "Arthur, meet Joe Fiebiger. He's a washed up third baseman and ironworker." That sure broke the ice. Sharp, an athlete and avid sports fan, and Klien obviously a sportsman and I talked about my other passion, baseball. Klien had already read our proposal and wanted to review the breakdown. I presented our schedule of overhead or shop burden. The "upset" amount of the proposal was $435,000 which included a contingency fund of $94,950. His eyes played over the numbers as Sharp and I sat quietly. He stopped reading, looked up at me and barked, "Advertising? You don't advertise!"

I smiled, "Yes we do. I buy a gross of golf balls every year with our company logo on them and give them as gifts."

He returned my smile, "I play golf."

"Would you like some golf balls?"

He nodded. Then, shifting to a more serious gear, he said, "The contingency fund has to go."

We agreed on a budgetary allowance of $350,000 and shook hands. The handshake was the contract. We received neither a signed contract nor a signed copy of our proposal. I didn't worry about it, the majority of the contracts for our work were verbal agreements. Once again I heard my father, "If you have a contract – you need a contract." Ninety two years, we were never in litigation.

Months later, Sharp was playing in a Platform Tennis tournament with me. As we chatted between matches, I asked, "Why did you guys never sign something that confirmed the proposal?"

"Why?" He asked. "We had faith in you. We didn't want to put pressure on you. We trusted you."

We built the new structure in a month. Then we moved all the stair parts from the museum and laid them out, being careful to allow room to navigate. The trial and error process of fitting sixteen hundred parts together had begun. No one ever said, "If only they had numbered the parts."

As Ranieri said, "It is what it is."

Cast iron had been proven to be structurally sound in both compression and tension in the late 1880s. Had Winslow Brothers' engineers not believed that the cast iron stringers would be strong enough support the stair? They chose to hedge their bets and wore belts and suspenders. They buried an iron bar into the beautiful cast iron stringers. The bar was five eighths of an inch thick and two and half inches wide and was riveted with ornamental rivets to the stringer.

The stringers had minor fissures--small cracks in the castings--either created at birth or a function of wear and tear. This required caution! Weintraub and his assistant, Wolcott, thought the process of magnetic particle inspection would accurately identify all defects. General Magnaplate Corporation was commissioned to perform this.

Their technicians applied colored, magnetic dies and then vibrated the work pieces with a magnetic field. The dies congregated at the blemishes and it revealed all, even the fractures that were seemingly invisible.

There were many, luckily none that violated the structural integrity of the various parts. There was no need to introduce the heat of welding. Buoyed by the belt and suspenders approach of the designers, we were free to treat the blemishes as minor. We arrested the progression of the break by drilling small holes at each extremity. We filled the voids with fine gauge copper wool.

We executed these tasks with relative ease. A larger problem lay ahead: the copper/iron interface. I called Joseph Karet, president and general manager of Keystone Plating, Inc. They had facilities both in Manhattan and Secaucus, New Jersey. I explained the issues to Karet. He listened and said, "You have to meet Richie Smith."

Meanwhile, Weintraub had enlisted the aid of archaeological metallurgist Martha Goodway. Goodway had graduated from MIT in 1957. She was on staff at the Smithsonian Institute and headed their laboratory at Kitty Hawk, North Carolina. She fit no preconceived prototypical mould of a lady scientist. Pretty in an understated way, she had high rosy cheekbones and an omnipresent smile. Always gracious and intent on everything being said, she was nonetheless the demur queen holding court. When she was deep in thought, you knew it. The gears in her eyes were going around.

Richard Smith, fifty-six, was an amazing man. He described his youth as "wild." He had toured the country by rail as a hobo. As a seventeen-year-old he was incarcerated for a short period of time. He discussed this event with great vigor, explaining, "I was just bored. I would never hurt anyone." He spent all of his available time in the library--he studied the sciences. He went on to graduate from Columbia University for both his undergraduate and postgraduate work. He established his science laboratory, Group Research, Inc. It took three floors of a building on Center Street in Manhattan. Group Research served the plating industry. Smith had patented new processes for plating and was one of three approved consultants for the airline industry.

Smith looked the prototypical image of a scientist. A shorter, less flamboyant version of the character, Doc, in *Back To The Future*. Slight of build, straight blond hair and smile a mile wide, he was not just an innovator – he was a problem solver. And he had a sense of humor. There was only one Richie Smith.

He, Weintraub and I became good friends. As Smith saved Sullivan's stair, he later saved the Statue of Liberty.

Late on an autumn day we all met for the first time in Smith's laboratories. Fluorescent lights humming, beakers boiling, small motors pumping solutions, vapors rising and timers alerting the completion of ongoing procedures. A working lab was now a lab full of geniuses: Goodway; Smith; and Weintraub.

Goodway and Smith formed a mutual admiration society, Goodway, gracious and modest, yet exalted, Smith humble and brilliant.

They, along with Weintraub, identified the problems: how to remove the existing copper plating; how to release the hydrogen embrittlement that had occurred; and how to plate again.

Sullivan Stair - Restored

American Wing - Metropolitan Museum of Art

1983

We decided to have a local Chinese restaurant deliver dinner rather than interrupt the proceedings. Too much was happening to have it aborted--even for moment.

Smith thought that micro-blasting with a mild abrasive agent should be the first step. We still blasted with sand in a controlled environment. Charcoal filtered air, fed through special headgear eliminated health hazards to the operator. We had developed a method of blasting with specific pressures and volumes of air that did not remove good material. Smith thought that walnut shells would be better. He was, as usual a few steps ahead, he wanted no silica residue to impede the mild pickling bath that would prepare the surfaces for the next phase. He described the pickling process, confirmed with Goodway and Karet the amounts of amperage per square inch that would be required.

Goodway, Smith and Weintraub discussed whether the stair had been in a hydrogen rich environment that could have subjected it to the vicissitudes of hydrogen embrittlement.

Simply put, some metals, iron in particular, when permeated by hydrogen may present a situation that greatly reduces the strength of the material. This causes failures of the body of work.

They agreed that no dice could be rolled here. Embrittled or not, the materials had to be treated as if they were compromised.

Smith and Goodway bantered about procedures to relieve the hydrogen embrittlement. They suggested and discarded a variety of ideas. The empty food containers stood sentry over the work benches. Time moved slowly. No one spoke. The beakers continued to simmer and the pumps hummed. A curious loud silence settled over us.

Then Smith said softly, "Orange Juice."

"What?" Asked Goodway with a rising voice.

"Orange Juice," Smith repeated. "Orange Juice at 400 degrees Fahrenheit for an hour." Goodway, at first expressionless, sat straight on the lab stool absorbed in her thoughts, suddenly beamed.

"Brilliant!" She said. She jumped off of her lab stool and danced a little jig, "It'll work."

Karet said, "I don't have tanks big enough."

Weintraub said, "Build 'em."

"Outa what?" Karet said.

Smith answered, "You can get three eighths of an inch thick polypropylene sheets big enough to make those tanks."

Karet nodded.

Second problem solved. Now on to the copper plating.

It was now past eight o'clock and Smith was still on a roll. He looked at Goodway and asked, "What would you think of electroless nickel followed by copper plate?"

"Why electroless nickel? Why not conventional electroplated nickel?"

"Less chance of future embrittlement."

They discussed the processes that had to be executed and how to proceed. Shop talk.

By nine o'clock they had solved three monumental scientific problems over a Chinese dinner in a science lab. I had been as silent as the empty Chinese food containers. What a treat to have been an observer.

---

Sullivan had designed ornate risers, vertical sections between the treads of a staircase. The risers had small horizontal shelves as part of their body, these supported the marble stair treads. The risers and stringers had tabs cast in them to allow

Post and Binder Fasteners, also referred to as "Sex Screws"

the mechanical fastenings of the risers to the stringers.

Another problem, Winslow Brothers thought that it was okay to literally put a square peg in a round hole. They used carriage bolts that have square shoulders and set them into the round holes to fasten the risers.

As they had at the Morgan Library, Industrial Fasteners Corporation came through again. Confronted with this situation they designed a post and binder screw. This type of fastener is often called a sex screw.

They copied the heads exactly and even made serrated shafts to the body of the female so that it could not twist.

The architects had designed larger balcony areas than Sullivan had. We enlarged the iron grilles and the decorative facias that covered the horizontal structural steel. Rather than tilt at another cast iron windmill, we made the facia extensions out of cast bronze. The original decorative details were maintained, the copper plating hid the bronze.

We erected the staircases, balconies, and stair railings for inspection. Again, a large entourage of museum staff, led by Sharp and Weintraub, attended. This time we not only added more water to the coffee, we bought a dozen new coffee cups. They inspected everything, walked up and down the stair, talked with the craftsmen. They were pleased with the work and were delighted to know the men who had done the work, had expended over ten thousand hours of labor, had indeed, enjoyed their tasks.

As we drank coffee and mingled, the two final questions came forward for debate. How to treat the "wobble" of the balcony railings and how to treat the patina. The enlargement of the balconies had naturally mandated that the length of the railings be extended. This extension caused them to vibrate when touched. Never in danger of collapsing, they were nonetheless unstable enough to frighten visitors. The railings needed supporting members along their length. These braces are called "raker braces."

I showed Sharp a sample of the raker braces that we had made a few years before for the fences at the East Front of The United States Capitol. They were forged in iron, provided great strength and were nondescript. But--they would introduce a non-Sullivan element into the mix. There were no Sullivan elements that could have been modified to provide this function. Sharp solved the problem quickly. He liked the forged braces and suggested that we incorporate them to be a stands for the labels. They would go unnoticed and would not even be considered a part of Sullivan's assemblage.

A much larger concern was the color for the patina. We leaned against benches, sat on lunch room stools and asked each other questions. Sullivan certainly knew the progression of copper colors. He knew that it started at the polished or satin color of copper and began the migration at the purplish tone of eggplant, then passed to the statutory color of assorted chocolates and finally arrived at the dullish green of verdigris. He knew that he could "jump start" nature by the application of chemicals and induce whatever patinated color he chose. But what had he chosen?

Some argued that he would have left it in its polished state, similar, as we discovered a few years later to August Bartholdi's approach to the State of Liberty. He might have liked the eggplant color, many do. Or the statuary softness of chocolate, or the softer verdigris.

Sharp looked at me and said, "Joe, you're being pretty quiet. What do you think?"

"I have this crazy fear. I think that some grandmotherly lady who had worked at The Chicago Stock Exchange is going to be in New York visiting her family. They're going to visit the museum. Come to the American Wing and this dear little old lady is going be enchanted to see the stair again. She'll climb it and then she will jump up and down, screaming, 'That's not the right color!'"

Bemused, Sharp said, "You sure have a way of putting things, Joe. So what do we do?"

We had multiple problems with application of a chemical patina. First, if the smell of the warm chemicals was picked up in the heating, ventilating and air conditioning system we could  tarnish all of the silver in the museum. This sounds alarming, but there were devices available to immediately exhaust the fumes and prevent this. Still it could be worrisome.

Unequivocally, we needed a reversible patina. We had always planned to provide the chosen color by applying different chemical recipes with heat. This process had some irreversibility with the patinist playing different recipes with different heats. Nonetheless, sometimes the modification required physical abrasion, i.e., sandpaper. Such physical abrasion was not acceptable.  That damn little old lady!

Not the loud silence of Smith's laboratory. The shop was humming with sounds of ironwork--hammers, saws, and welding. Grinding had been halted.

"Any suggestions?" Asked Weintraub?

"Faux stuff. Crazy stuff, cheating stuff. Stuff you really don't want to know about?" I said.

Everyone was listening and I was embarrassed. "We can use metal powders. Set them in a binder of *Banana Oil* or *French Bronzing Liquid* and make it look like the chemical patina. We can fool you."

Weintraub asked, "Is it reversible?"

"Lacquer thinner."

Curator, Craig Miller, smiled yet said with a sarcastic tone, "Do you do this often?"

"Only in emergencies."

I went to Opa's old metal cabinet. Had it been given a name it would have been "Cabinet of Special Finishes." Here resided an old cache of finishing stuff. The cabinet was speckled with many decades of overspray. Doors that didn't want to budge and locks though not locked that didn't want to release. The doors groaned, but they opened. Inside were finely ground metal powders in ancient tin containers, gold leaf, silver leaf, aluminum leaf, red gilder's clay, gold size and the ever popular, rabbit skin glue (used for laying gold leaf). There were also some fresh bottles of *French Bronzing Liquid* and *Banana Oil.* I brought out copper, brass, bronze, and aluminum powders. Ranieri made a little tool with which to pry open these ancient tops.

We played, mixing different powders in the different binders and applying them to extra stair parts. Voila! Any color, any blending of colors any texture that the staff requested could be stumbled upon. This was a definite "maybe."

A dark bronze color mixed with lighter tones was chosen. That color would have been about twenty years into the life of stair. It was a pleasing finish, it was reversible. It still remains. My imaginary old lady never showed up.

As an aside, all knowledgeable metal and wood finishers use these powders and binders to either make or repair finishes. I had even seen some finishers mix the powders into a lacquer base and apply it by spray. It is deemed, "A trick of the trade." To clean delicate finishes (i.e., patinas, gold leaf, gold plate, etc.) one should use *Oil of Lavender* or mild lemon oil. Apply it to cheesecloth and wipe gently.

There had been many changes to the scope of the project since its inception. A natural function would have been to increase our budget allowance. Some semblance of good business practices required that we document these events. Additions to the original scope of work had increased, and the original budget had grown commensurately. But that money was never needed.

Smiles all around. Sharp, ebullient as he described this said, "Now we can do the other projects that we wanted to do." We saved approximately $75,000 on one project and they found $200,000 for us to participate with the restorations of The Tiffany loggia; Vanderbilt Fireplace; Pulpit with Sounding Board; Frank Lloyd Wright living room from a house in Wayzta, Minnesota; and made patinated bronze pedestals for sculptures.

The museum had a party with wine and canapés, for all of the staff, artisans and tradesmen who had worked on the American Wing project. The men received thanks for their "labors of love" from the museum staff. They had a second party to inaugurate the new wing, a black tie affair on a warm May evening in 1980. How we enjoyed the art, company, champagne and hors d'œuvres.

When I read the label on the wall at the Sullivan Stair I was amazed that it only stated that it had been restored, was the work of Louis Sullivan, and came from the Chicago Stock Exchange.

You would have thought that it was tomato plant that had been transplanted.

I kidded Sharp, "You make it sound like all you had to do was water it and just grew there."

He just smiled.

The American Wing ended and we began the Rockefeller Wing. Michael C. Rockefeller had died while acquiring this collection of African art. The sad rumor was that Rockefeller had been murdered by the natives after one of the two Evinrude outboard motors that he had given them failed to start.

We were enlisted to make the mounts for the unusually shaped art objects. We set up a little "rolling shop" in the museum. Here Ranieri and Karhut laid out the methods that we would use. Then Karhut and Giacomo Novielli cold forged all of the mounts. Then, with museum staff at the ready, the objects were mounted.

The Paintings Conservation Department had special easels that were loved by the restoration artists. The original easels had been made in France, circa 1795.

The museum had given a contract to have the original easels replicated. The contractor duplicated the wood exactly. But he failed to make the mechanisms work. The easels either would not rise or would rise and then fall. One artist was injured when his easel collapsed.

We duplicated the original mechanisms and fit them to the new woodwork. Locomotion for the originals was based upon a large threaded rod passing through a matching female gear. The type of thread is called an "acme" thread. Today you will commonly find these in workshop vises.
We had the rods and gear housings machined and replaced the defective ones. Once again we used our "rolling shop" and Karhut did the retrofitting *in situ*.

The Henry R. Luce Center for the Study of American Art is downstairs in the American Wing. It is treasure trove of American paintings and artifacts. The museum had installed what seemed like miles of glass and steel, full height--environmentally controlled display cases. The cases were to display paintings, sculpture, furniture and other heavy art objects.

We were to make the infrastructure to which the objects would be mounted, either directly or by brackets. Certainly not art themselves, but the adjustable features that were mandated required arithmetic discipline, strength, accuracy and invisibility.

We had thousands of one half inch diameter holes to drill and thread. The center-to center-dimension had to be exactly two inches. Ranieri, always brilliant made a *drill jig* that complied with this restriction--within reason. Expending vast amounts of labor, using modern, albeit non computerized machinery, we managed to control this arithmetic "creep."

Phase I was completed and everything worked well. It had been a very expensive endeavor. The labor expended certainly was not artistic, just highly disciplined.

I knew that Phase II would mimic Phase I. There had to be a less expensive way to do this.

I called my good friend Gerson Feiner, President and General Manager of P. Feiner and Sons, Inc., a large metal fabricating company in Bogota, New Jersey. Feiner said that his machine shop had a new CNC (computerized) machine, that could drill and tap these holes in a fraction of the time. There was a zero error tolerance. Good bye arithmetic creep. Feiner quoted a price for Phase II that was exponentially less than Phase I. The two phases were identical.

This information was happily received by museum staff, but not by Iron Workers Local #455. Our shop was a family shop. Every man knew that he had a job fifty-two weeks a year, year in, year out. We never laid off. The union called us a "country club." The coffee pot was always on. If an employee had a death in the family, he was paid for his bereavement time. If he had jury duty he was paid. If it snowed and he was late, he was paid. Our men were paid higher wages than the union scale. The company was the men. Their welfare reflected on the company's welfare.

Fortunately, with God's good grace, we always had work. The responsibility that we had for the men was also vested in our responsibilities to both our clients and our art. It was a multi-faceted covenant that had worked relatively well.

The Metropolitan Museum was certainly a prime client. We owed it to them to save them money where we could. I authorized Feiner to proceed with drilling of the holes. Union president, William Colovito had been advised of this and was determined to stop it.

He came to the shop as he always did, unannounced, with the silence of a cat burglar. He expected whatever was in progress to be halted so that he could have center stage. He was soft spoken and usually immovable. He sat and said, "What's this I heard about a job at the museum?" He always spoke softly, I leaned forward and said, "What did you say?" He repeated it and added, "That's a loss of work for 'my men.'"

"What loss? There is no loss of work," I countered.

He argued, "You should have added more men."

"Bill," I said, "we have a responsibility to our clients. There was no loss of work. Has there ever been a loss of work?"

Grudgingly, with eyes that never met mine, he walked away.

Phase II was completed. The museum had saved many thousands of dollars.

As usual, they found more commissions for us.

The men loved working at the Met. We were called in one day to solve a major problem with the pivoting of a heavy door. When Ranieri and I arrived, I heard a curator say, "Thank God, Bruno's here."

Before committing ourselves to the Statue of Liberty, I asked Sharp for his blessing. The Statue of Liberty commission would come and go, but the Met's commissions would always be there. He was pleased that I had asked.

"Don't worry, we'll work it out."

# Chapter 19
## Mary B.D.T. Semans

The entrance to the Metropolitan Museum of Art is at eighty-second street and Fifth Avenue. Directly across Fifth Avenue, staring directly at the Museum entrance is the six story residence, 1009 Fifth Avenue. Architect Alexander MacMillan Welch designed it for developers William and Thomas Hall. They sold it to the brothers Duke.

Benjamin N. Duke and his brother James B. Duke made the family fortune with American Tobacco Company. They lived in Durham, North Carolina and were the founders of Duke University.

James Duke, with his family moved into the mansion in Manhattan in 1909. He moved out in 1912 when other family members, Anthony J. Drexel Biddle, Jr. and his wife, Mary, Benjamin's daughter moved in. They maintained residences in New York City, Irvington, New York in Westchester County and Durham.

Forged iron finials, copper balustrade and copper frieze

They enlisted the architectural and interior design talents of Karl Bock for all of their residences and Duke University. Bock, born in Stuttgart, Germany had studied in the University of Basel, Switzerland. He immigrated to the U.S. in 1912 at the age of twenty-four. Bock was the founder of the American Institute of Decorators, now the American Society of Interior Designers.

Bock's designs were in the French styles and ventured to the modern. He was a man for all architectural and decorative seasons. Opa and Dad were always making something of Bock's design for the Biddle families as well as his other clients.

One of those clients was New York State Governor Herbert H. Lehman. Bock designed a large aluminum and copper dining room table and chairs for him. Aluminum was in its infancy. Bock designed friezes with motifs of fruits and leaves. The friezes were made as repoussé pieces, hammered into a base of warm pitch.

The galvanic reaction of two dissimilar metals called for an interface. The copper friezes were gold plated and an acceptable balance of nobility was achieved.

After Lehman's death, the furniture was often found at the auctions of Parke Benet or Christies. Under the guidance of Craig Miller and Lewis Sharp it finally found its way, to the American Wing of the Metropolitan Museum of Art.

Opa and Bock had a relationship of business and friendship. Both German immigrants who had learned to speak English well, they nonetheless only spoke German to each other. Not only did they often dine together, they had a common love of horse racing. They often studied the racing forms together. Opa had a bookie and placed the wagers for both of them.

The Bocks would often visit for spring and summer barbecues at our New Rochelle home. The first Saturday in May, horse racing's, "Run

For The Roses," was a special day. Opa provided the spirits, Mrs. Bock the pastries and Mom the heavy German dishes. Oh how I hated that food.

They would have mint juleps and make their picks. Bock's choices were often slanted as he had clients whose horses were in the race. Once decided, Opa would make a phone call. Then they would gather in front of black and white television and watch the race.

I was, in the eyes of Bock, the essence of Teutonic primogeniture; the first male born into a German family of metal workers. As such, he always treated me kindly and he always sought to teach me something. He was just "Mr. Bock" to me. I never realized how famous he was.

During one of these summer barbecues my father and Bock were exchanging stories. Dad had taken a crew of men to Durham to install a curved stair railing. Smoking cigarettes was common then, they kept little ashtrays on the steps as they worked. My father and all of the men smoked Lucky Strike cigarettes, a product of American Tobacco. Whether the men had been asked to smoke Luckies or not was never clear. But they left packages on the stairs next to the ash trays.

Mrs. Biddle walked the stairs and inspected the work, she spied the Luckies and said to my father, "They're horrible, why don't you smoke something else?"

Always the gentlemen, my father replied, "We like them."

Dad said that she smiled graciously and continued down the stairs, smoking what he believed was a Chesterfield, made by competitor, Liggett & Meyers.

Bock and Opa had not heard the story and great laughter abounded around the wines, pig's knuckles, sauerkraut, bratwursts and salad.

Fortunately the Teutonic Bill of Fare was sometimes forgotten in the name of "lobster." Dad had a friend who had a business of trucking lobsters from Maine to New York. Many, many times lobsters were barbecued in the coals, barbecued on the rack or whatever the chef of day imagined might be nice. It didn't matter, it was lobster.

We were often invited to watch the Columbus Day parade, march down Fifth Avenue. We gathered on the roof in the enveloped by the safety of the copper balustrade. We dressed warmly and Mrs. Biddle served hot apple cider and pastries.

Unfortunately Mrs. Bock suffered a mild stroke in the late 1950s. She was confined to a wheelchair and getting into and out of the car was extremely difficult. Bock asked my father if he had any suggestions.

Dad didn't blink, "Leave the car with me, we'll come up with something."

He designed a pivoting, sliding, lockable seat and even devised a seat belt long before they came into common use. He obtained the seat belt from an aircraft supplier. The sliding seat required no electric motors, no hydraulic cylinders, just mechanical glides, gears, bushings and bearings.

Mary Biddle Duke Semans, daughter of Mary Biddle took over the houses after her mother's death in 1960. They enlisted the talents of preservation and restoration architect Gerald Allen to create a master plan for the restoration of the building.

Allen was born and raised in North Carolina. He was a graduate of Yale University's School of Architecture and often returned as a visiting critic. His quick darting eyes, smile, wit and grace fit the image of the Southern Gentleman. I always believed that his sensitivities, talents and listening skills, coupled with the unbridled attention to the details of his work made him a special talent. And he was a likeable guy.

Semans and her son, James, loved 1009 Fifth Avenue. They wanted it restored in accordance with Allen's all encompassing master plan. The copper mansard roof with its balustrades had to be removed, replicated precisely and re-installed. The iron and glass marquee also had to be removed, restored and refitted with laminated safety glass. The cast iron bay window required disassembly, repair and re-glazing with safety glass. All of the iron window grilles and exterior railings called for attention. Finally, the building's masonry work had to be re-pointed and waterproofed.

There was decorative copper work and decorative sheet metal work. The sheet metal repairs were simplistic and easy. The copper was not.

The copper pieces were made by Miller and Doing Company, Brooklyn, New York. Our company library had their catalog, Sheet Metal Ornament, Volume K. The elements were called *rope stampings*. The stampings were used for decorative ceilings, cornices, and many other types of ornament. They were made of twenty-four gauge copper (.021"), slightly more than one sixty-fourth of an inch thick or approximately three strands of human hair. Their strength came from the depressions, both convex and concave as well as the angle bends which were imparted to them. This was a popular method which began in 1880s. It was found on many buildings, including Ellis Island.

William Van Alen, architect for the Chrysler Building designed his terraced crown of arches. He pioneered, using the precursor for stainless steel. He engaged German metal manufacturer, Krupp, and used their *Nirosta*, which was a German acronym that meant "rust proof steel." In America it was called *Monel* and was the forerunner for stainless steel.

My good friend, noted high altitude, climbing photographer, Peter B. Kaplan was the only photographer given permission to climb the world's tallest free standing scaffold. It was erected by Universal Building Supply, Inc. and Brisk Waterproofing for the Restoration of Crown of the Chrysler Building from 1980-1981. Krupp's *Nirosta* had not failed. The Chrysler Building had suffered the same electrolytic fate as the Statue of Liberty. The armature and mechanical connections were iron. They, being less noble than the German material had rusted. At the mercy of the winds, the skin tore and warped.

Kaplan scaled its heights from the outside by climbing the scaffolding. The workers who repaired and replaced the two hundred seventeen feet of

*Nirosta* befriended him. The original cap was replaced, the old one was given to Kaplan as a token of friendship. Kaplan has this piece in his studio. I studied it with great interest. There were no similar imperfections. Closing out his collection are the interior *Nirosta* wall sconces.

Kaplan was also the preferred photographer for the Statue of Liberty/ Ellis Foundation. All of the copper pieces of Ellis Island were twenty-four gauge copper. They failed in the late 1970s because of their thinness and because the rips, wrinkles and tears. These were a natural consequence of *rope stamping*. The copper elements of the Mansard and balustrades of 1009 Fifth Avenue failed for the same reasons.

The work on the Chrysler Building had been executed via the repoussé process by Kenneth Lynch and Sons of Wilton, Connecticut.

The following is part of an article written by Kenneth Lynch, Sr., for one of his company's catalogs.

*"...HISTORICAL DATA ABOUT ROPE DROP STAMPINGS AND REPOUSSÉ WORK*

*The "rope drop stamping" business seems to have been started in France in a small way towards the end of the 17th century.*

*The French are very famous for their repoussé ornament all done by hand. In searching for a way to produce similar work the "rope drop" stamping system was discovered.*

*Basically a water wheel was involved which turned a shaft continuously and on this shaft was a wheel or a drum and wrapped around this drum two or three times was a piece of stout rope and when the hammer man applied a little pressure on the rope, he*

Rope Stamping at an aviation plant

*could raise the hammer, and upon releasing it, the hammer would fall and a stamping would begin.*

*Really to call this work stamping would be incorrect for these ornaments are actually hammered as it took considerable skill on the part of the hammer man to nurse the metal down into the die and many of these men were very clever indeed. This system was used for the making of ornaments used on the mansard roofed buildings and it was basically a zinc and copper business.*

*The buildings in France at that time were made largely of stone and all of the stone ornaments had to be carried up and tremendous supporting members had to be introduced to connect the stone ornament.*

*There being many modelers and sculptors available in France, they soon found that by the use of this hammering system a stone ornament could be duplicated in zinc or copper and painted appropriately and a whole new industry was discovered and developed.*

*With the invention of a hand tool known as a "bible" probably because it looked like a little book - these hammered pieces were fitted to the buildings so that the cornice work all made of sheet metal replaced the old stone brackets and modillions.*

*The silversmiths were quick to find the advantage in this system because they began to use it for the rough shaping of bowls and ornamental work and in three countries this method of forming persisted for nearly 100 years. These countries were France, England and the United States of America.*

*In France this work is still done on an important scale and the writer still has strong contacts with two companies there.*

*In England there are at least three entire shops that are devoted to nothing but this work.*

*In the United States of America there was at the turn of the century about two dozen shops doing this work and some of these shops had as many as 100 employees. However, these shops only did architectural work and the real big use for these old hammers was in the silver industry and firms like International Silver, The Gorham Company, Wallace*

*Silversmiths and others just to mention a few, used this equipment until about 1950. However, in the silver industry they used wide belts over the pulleys instead of ropes. ..."*

I explained this history to Allen and Semans. Lynch had acquired Miller and Doing, but they were not making *rope stampings* in 1983. There had to be a way to make these thousands of pieces and I had to find it. Both Allen and James Semans wanted to be active participants in this process.

I went to Rex Forge in Plantsville, Connecticut, a large drop forging facility. They did not do *rope stampings* any more but they did have used machinery for sale. I toured their plant and watched as they manufactured drop forged hammer heads for The Stanley Corporation. The percussion made the building shake and the lights flicker. The noise generated seemed to be louder than a jet.

The talented workmen were dressed with safety equipment for good reasons. They had to control the speed of the falling die. Too fast, and it would break both itself and its mating die, too slow and not enough power would be generated to make the hammer head. They controlled this speed with the tension that they applied to the ropes that released the head.

This factory setting was surreal. Oil fired the forges to heat the iron were next to each machine. The smell hung in the dark air. Lighting was minimal in order for the workers to determine the heat of the iron by its color. The sound was deafening. The vibrations frightening. If there were a *Dante's Inferno* for manufacturing, this was it. This was a *rope stamping/ drop forging* process and I was in shock.

It required a machine approximately fifteen feet tall, that weighed four tons, registering an unknown number on the Richter scale and created a higher decibel count louder than a jet airplane.

I knew that there was no way that I could bring this monster into mid Manhattan.

I studied this with fascination and asked my guide, over the noise, "Is there a more modern version?"

"Not that's any quieter or doesn't shake."

I shook my head, shook his hand, thanked him and fled the building.

Balinda and the kids had accompanied me on this trip. I had the good sense to not expose them to this lack of Industrial Hygiene. I got in the car and Balinda knew that I was confused.

She said, "You can feel the ground shake out here and you can hear it, too. What are you going to do?" She knew, that monster wasn't coming into our shop.

"This is 1983, there has to be a better way. I'll find it."

The first thing that came to mind on the ride home was, hydraulics.

I visited the manufacturer of large hydraulic presses in Clifton, New Jersey. Modern Hydraulics, Inc. was managed by its owner, Nick Brodsky. A huge man with a walrus mustache, he looked intimidating but was really a gentle giant.

I explained my predicament and showed him a few of the pieces that we had to fabricate. The pieces had multiple peaks and valleys. He didn't like the peaks and valleys part of it. Deep drawing the material was easy, navigating the multiple surfaces was hard.

He had manufactured the *triple acting hydraulic presses* that coffee pot manufacturer, West Bend, used. West Bend's factory was nearby. Brodsky called, spoke with foreman and asked if he could bring a visitor.

West Bend's plant floor had thirty or more of Brodsky's presses. They are *triple acting* because they have two hydraulic cylinders, one above, one below and the *coup de grâce*, a third cylinder that is an air cushion.

The foreman walked me through the process. They had one eighth of an inch aluminum blanks prepared. A "slippery" wax like agent, then unknown to me was applied to the piece. An operator placed it over iron rings around the perimeter and the top cylinder descended slowly and quietly and with no percussive force. The only noise heard was the aluminum stretching. It sounded like a cat when someone stepped on its tail.

The material had been held lightly in place by the perimeter rings. The lower rings were attached via rods to the surfaces of the upper and lower cylinders. Their attachment to the lower hydraulic cylinder was interrupted by the air cylinder. The upper die, moved slowly and steadily forced the migration of the aluminum into the female cavity. Somewhere between eight and ten pounds of air pressure were required for the air cushion. This was an empirical phase. The unknown element was the critical lubricating agent. It allowed the material to "slip" while it is being coaxed to its shape. This process, minus the peaks and valleys, required only one pass and no annealing. The process took thirty seconds.

There were no tears, the wrinkles only appeared on the areas that would be cut off.

The foreman looked at the peaks and valleys of my piece. "Not impossible. It'll take some playing around. Keep adjusting the heights of the rods. You'll get it. Can I call you Joe?"

"Sure."

"Maybe you could have made these as mechanical stampings. But you would have had the same problems. You would have soldered patches over the rips."

"But they still make fireman's helmets like this, don't they?"

"Larger radii, they don't have to be pretty, only strong. You'll get this," he continued, "adjust the heights of the rods in small increments, file here, file there. It'll let you do the peaks and valleys. Oh yeah, don't forget the 'Johnson's 7000.' Buy it by the case."

Brodsky was smiling. He had a sale.

"Can I ask you another question?"

"Sure."

"Why do you have so many of these machines?"

He paused, grinned, scratched his head and finally said, "Its cheaper to buy more machines from this guy than to have to knock them down and set them up again. Once you have it right, you don't want to lose it. Oh, by the way, keep a notebook near the machines, write everything down. You'll thank me for that."

The four post press was approximately ten feet tall, weighted two tons, created neither noise nor vibration. It was at its apex of technology for 1983. But to get the desired result one still needed a magic potion, Johnson's 7000. To this day I don't know what it does. I only know that it is magic.

This is explained in chapter eight of *Go Figure*.

I discussed all of this with Allen and Semans. They were pleased that we could make all of these pieces out of much heavier gauge material. Technology allowed us to reproduce the pieces without reproducing their fragility. A hundred years into the future the process would not need to be repeated.

We began our empirical journey and perfected the process of *deep drawing across multiple surfaces*. Plaster reproductions, both male and female were made by Fred Helbing. He allowed for shrinkage and had the plaster patterns cast in an aluminium alloy, *Kirksite*. The *kirksite* dies were highly polished in order to reduce friction. The new pieces were two and half times (.051") thicker than the originals. As such they were independent chassis, requiring no armatures. It took six "hits" of the press to coax the material safely to the bottom of the dies. In between each "hit" the copper had to be annealed to restore its soft properties. The imperfections that were inherent in the process were all outside of the usable areas and were trimmed away.

Once again the discussion of what the patinated color of the new work should had to addressed. Whatever the original architects had in mind was not considered. After eighty-three years the copper on the old work had migrated to the end of its spectrum, verdigris. Allen chose to allow the new copper to begin the migration process at nature's pace. The conventional wisdom of the '80s was that in New York City, the copper would reach the end of the spectrum in approximately fifteen years. It began its journey with a polished finish and moved to the purplish tint of "eggplant." Then it went to the soft chocolate color of statuary. It has held its statuary color for twenty-seven years. When it reaches verdigris is still to be determined.

The copper work completed, we began the straightforward restorations of the marquee, bay window, window grilles, doors and railings.

The restoration received the *1986 Chairman's Award for Excellence* from the *New York Landmarks Conservancy*. Allen, James Semans and our firm were sited for excellence.

On September 26, 1985, Joseph Giovannini wrote in *New York Times*, "The Wraps Come Off A 1901 Beaux Arts Mansion."

"Mr. Allen discovered the original drawings for the house in the Avery Library at Columbia University, which proved to be of some help in the restoration. The drawings showed, for example, that the building had six wrought-iron finials at the peaks of the roof. The architect re-created the finials from the drawings; executed by the Fiebiger company, they were presented as a gift by the company to the family - an Old World custom between artisan and patron, according to Mr. Fiebiger. A crane will install the 9-foot-high, 250-pound pieces in the next several weeks."

Once again, all of God's good graces were shining on us. Five years later we refined the process of deep drawing. We enlisted Modern Hydraulics to enhance the machinery, and developed a space age method of tooling. We stopped using *kirksite* and experimented with different polymers for the male and female dies. This empirical information helped us restore all of the decorative copper on the roof and domes of the Main Building on Ellis Island.

As an aside, the Semans' sold their 1009 Fifth Avenue home in 2006 for forty million dollars. The sale was said by realtors to be second highest price ever for a single family dwelling in Manhattan. It was sold again in 2009 for fifty million.

# Chapter 20
## Donald J. Trump, Trump Tower Residence

Donald J. Trump leaves an impression on everyone. His energetic, seemingly omnipresent high profile is part of our daily lives. Everyone seems to have an opinion about him. I grew to know him in the artistic side of business. I saw the veneer that everybody saw. Beneath the veneer was, in my opinion a charming, friendly, talented man. As I grew to understand him, I saw that one of his greatest talents were his listening skills.

He was a tall, physically fit, blond haired man with an ever present graceful flair. His glass walled office, sometimes surrounded by low clouds was filled with an eclectic blend. Some period furniture and an ultra modern polished metal and glass desk. He sat behind it in a relaxed manner, surveying all.

He surrounded himself with talented personnel and he heard what they said. He didn't always follow their advice, but he sure listened.

His was the first and only commission in my career where I felt that I had not fulfilled the desires of my client. He wanted something that did not exist at that time. He described what he wanted as something born in the ultra modern of style of Las Vegas. But it didn't even exist there, yet.

Explaining his

Louis XVI stair railings

quest to his architects, interior decorators and me was like describing blue to a blind man. I thought that he was trying to achieve the spender of Versailles in waters yet to be charted.

One of the architects in the group was a disciple of Mies van der Rohe. He frequently quoted the famous architect's aphorism, "Less is more." Trump wanted "more was more."

We designed and fabricated sweeping and graceful stair railings for the curved stair. A stylized, eclectic blend of the Louis XVI period was born. We hoped to compliment the stunningly beautiful idyllic Renaissance murals that adorned the walls.

We forged iron scrolls, hammered repoussé copper leaves, cast bronze pearl bars, made custom bronze moldings for the handrail and stair stringers, and cast bronze ionic columns for newel posts.

The sweep of the stair was so dynamic that it had its own personality. The railing was finished with twenty-three karat gold leaf and polished bronze moldings. You can be the judge. It was elegant and sumptuous, but I think that it never achieved the affect that Trump desired.

Trump never told this to me. I think that he just accepted that he was far ahead of his time.

One day while discussing our continuing fight to get the motif right, he asked, "Can you design a Trump monogram for the railing?"

"Do you mean that bock letter 'T'?"

"No, something more in keeping with the design. Has it been done before?" He concluded.

I was quiet while I thought.

"Only Marie Antoinette comes to mind. *The Petit Trianon*," I said.

He wrinkled his nose and said, "Forget it."

He was caught, I thought, in between the Never Never Land of classical beauty and the new modern world of glass, mirror, marble and polished metals.

He respected the talents and the large amount of labor being expended to produce a beautiful piece. But, something was missing.

He had asked, through his project manager, John D'Allesio, whether the entire railing, could be gold plated.

I once again called upon the genius of Richie Smith. Smith said that it could be done. Like the Sullivan Stair at the Metropolitan Museum, new tanks would have to be made. The process was not complicated. It just needed huge baths. Smith gave a estimate.

At my next meeting with Trump, he asked, "Well, what do think? Can we gold plate the whole thing?"

"Yes," I said to his smiling eyes.

"How much will it cost?"

"Four hundred thousand dollars."

"Not as bad a I thought. Let's try the gold leaf first. If I don't like it, then we'll plate it."

Trump liked the gold leaf and all thoughts of gold plating were dismissed.

We also made very large chandeliers. The perimeters of the chassis for the fixtures required four inch wide brass. Cast bronze acanthus leaves for a frieze were mounted on the top of the band. Thousands of one quarter inch diameter balls were mounted, like pearls, in borders running parallel with the upper and lower edges of the chassis. Hand cut Russian crystals were attached and became the focal point of each fixture.

P. Feiner and Sons, Inc. punched the holes in the chassis with their computerized equipment. This assured the much needed precision for mounting the balls and crystals. Then everything was gold plated.

The balls were fastened to the chandelier with screws that were smaller than raisins. Each ball touched the next. There wasn't much room for adult hands. We tried using tweezers, but they scratched the gold plating.

We decided to have a kid's party in the shop. Balinda invited our kid's friends to a party. The kids were paid and fed as they, with their small hands, wearing light cotton gloves, installed thousands of Donald Trump's gold balls.

We followed up with few utilitarian, nondescript tasks and the commission ended pleasantly.

# Chapter 21
## Restoration of the Statue of Liberty

By and large, native New Yorkers never went to the Empire State Building or the Statue of Liberty, except for on class trips in elementary school. Like the great pastrami sandwich you can get a three o'clock in the morning at the Stage Deli, it's great to know it's there, but you'll use it another time.

So it was for me until I heard rumors that the green lady in the harbor needed major repairs.

My wife Balinda, blonde, blue eyes, five foot seven, fine of figure has always been the proverbial "girl next door." She is the Will Rogers of books, "...she never met a book that she didn't like. ..." We briefly talked about a family trip to the Statue. Bingo, she had been to the library and had a collection of historical, architectural and kids books. She read them and made copious notes.

On a warm day in late May 1983 we made a family trip. Balinda, Beth, ten and Paul, three and me. We drove down the West Side highway as Balinda read her notes.

"France wanted to help America celebrate her one hundredth birthday. A French diplomate, Édouard Laboulaye," she stopped to slowly pronounce it in French. "Laboulaye wanted to salute freedom and Lincoln's abolishment of slavery."

Beth interrupted, "France didn't have slaves did they, Mom?"

"You're right, they didn't have slaves. But they didn't want one guy telling them what to do."

"A monarchy?" Beth quizzed.

"Yes, dear, a monarchy."

"Laboulaye had a dinner party at his house outside Versailles in 1865. I wish I knew the exact date. Lincoln was assassinated on April 14th, I wonder if they met after that. Laboulaye talked about a gift to America to celebrate *liberty* and the end of slavery. A sculptor was there, Frédérick Auguste Bartholdi. He got caught up in the idea and wanted to design it."

We parked and took the ferry to the statue. As we approached the dock Balinda said to the kids, "Look at her, her torch is 305 feet high."

"Are we going up in it?" Beth asked.

"Only as far as the head. They closed the torch in 1916 after an explosion."

We entered the granite pedestal. "Where are we?" Asked Beth.

"They wanted to use the statue as a lighthouse so they put her up high. We're on the ground floor now." We entered a large elevator and Balinda continued, "This will take us up 155 feet to the base of the statue. Then we'll climb."

We exited the elevator and entered the ingenious double decker spiral stair and climbed to the top. We were in a group as we slowly inched upward. The stair was steep and Paul's little legs had to work hard. He asked, "How many are there?"

"Three hundred fifty-four."

I marveled at the network of twisted and shaped iron armature bars. They looked like noodles in a Chinese restaurant. No two were alike. Something was wrong though, many of the rivets that held them in place were missing.

We finally arrived at the crown. As we walked past twenty-five windows, Balinda said, "Right above us are the seven spikes. They are the rays of sunshine for seven continents." We enjoyed the beautiful panorama of Manhattan and the river traffic. Gently the crowd eased us to our descent.

I said to no one in particular, "All that climbing for thirty seconds?"

By the time we got to ground level, everyone was hungry and thirsty. We went to the cafeteria and gift shop; I bought lunch; Balinda bought books and a small replica of the lady. We ate and studied the pictures and the model.

Beth saw the spikes and chains in a book, she pointed at them and said, "Why didn't we get to see these?"

I didn't have an answer. Yet.

Satisfied with food, drink and rest we continued our field trip. We brought binoculars and took turns looking up. Beth asked, "Who do you think she's supposed to be?"

Balinda said, "Some people think that Bartholdi chose his wife, others say his mother."

Balinda pulled her notes out of her purse and began reading. "She was made in a Paris workshop." Bilingual with French, she stopped to teach it, "its called *atelier*."

"The *atelier* of Gaget, Gauthier and Company did the metal work. They had over fifty men. Their foreman was Marie Simon"

"Was it a company likes yours, Daddy?" Beth asked.

"Much bigger," I answered.

"Was Simon like Bruno?" She continued.

"Probably," I said, "but he had to have a lot help."

"They made the right arm and torch first and displayed them in the 1876 Philadelphia World's Fair. People paid fifty cents to climb to the top of the observation deck. It was the beginning of fund raising. After Bartholdi made the model, there were thirty thousand calculations needed to enlarge it.

Supposedly over 300,000 men, women and children visited the *atelier* of Gaget and Gauthier. Monsieur Gaget made small scale models of the statue in plaster. These replicas came to be known in English as "gadgets."

*Construction of the Pedestal*

"They were great money raiser," Balinda continued.

"No kidding," I said. "And they still are. Look at what you bought."

The day was done, we walked to the pier. I lingered and looked up at her, my mind wandered. I was caught between two aphorisms, "If you stand still you go backwards" and "Don't let the Tiger grab by the tail." If I got involved, would I land on my feet?

I heard Balinda bellowing, "If you don't hurry, you'll miss the boat!"

I came back to planet Earth and went to join them. Tired and dirty we boarded the boat, enjoyed the sights of Manhattan and went home.

Thirty-three year old sculptor Frédérick Auguste Bartholdi was granted his wish to fulfill the dreams of statesmen Édouard René de Lefèbrve Laboulaye. Bartholdi began his designs immediately. Was the model his wife, his mother, or the recent widow of sewing machine inventor, Issac Singer? No one was sure.

His quest was to show power, grace, dignity and beauty. He raised the heel of her right foot as if to gracefully walk forward and greet the sons and daughters of liberty. Broken chains, a beautiful face and a torch fulfilled his artistic messages.

Work began at the Paris *atelier* of Gaget, Gauthier and Company in the winter of 1875. Though a gift from France, the French raised funds in America twice. Their first successful attempt was 1876 in Philadelphia. They continued to succeed when the head and shoulders were displayed at the Paris World's Fair in June 1878. Bartholdi was enchanated with the idea of visitors ascending the interior to be rewarded with remarkable vistas. They enjoyed the experience and a new wrinkle was added to the his repertoire.bugler

In 1880, ten years before his famous tower, Gustav Eiffel designed one of architecture's first *curtain walls* for the Statue. The skin did not carry any weight other than its own. It transferred all wind loads back to the structural steel pylons. While he harnessed the wind he also allowed the body to follow the sun's journey through the southern sky.

Richard Morris Hunt was commissioned to design the base. The first American to graduate from the École des Beaux-Arts he was the founder of the American Institute of Architects,

Work on the pedestal was often interrupted as fund raising started and stopped. Joseph Pulitzer, publisher of the *New York World* offered to print the name of every benefactor in his newspaper. Even those who contributed only a penny had their names printed and received a commemorative lapel pin. It was magic. Funds poured in and the pedestal was completed in April 1886.

History seems to have passed over Gaget's foreman. Marie Simon. He is seen in many photos and was a traveling companion of Bartholdi. Simon was in charge of all phases of the work. Bartholdi named him in his will to carry on in the event of his untimely death.

Mathematically enlarged, the points in space were fitted to wood forms and plaster forms backed with lath. Woodworkers cut slices of wood to match the profiles of the plaster. Trial and error, fitting after fitting, these "cat scan" like wood pieces were joined with iron tie rods. Once the negative impressions were completed, the hammering began. The copper was from France's mines in Visney, Norway. The sheets were 99.9% pure (inferior grades approximate 99.75%) and were three-thirty-seconds of an inch thick, the approximate thickness when holding a dime and penny together. They were coaxed into shape by hammering. Sometimes the hammers were of hardened steels, sometimes rawhide, sometimes wood. Downward hammering always thins the material.

The pieces were *work hardened* (rendered brittle) by the hammering. How did they restore the original properties, a process termed annealing? Some historians referred to the use of an oxygen-acetylene torch. Others say the pieces were returned to the forge.

Oxygen and acetylene torches did not arrive in the American workshop for another twenty years. And then, curiously it's birth was in tablet form, not the compressed gas of today.

Gaget was remarkably clever. He designed a system where two boards, each with rounded edges were pivoted at their extremities, an ingenious yet rudimentary tool that served as an adjustable bending brake. It folded the copper of the robes. The robes maintained their original thickness. They are by definition, bent sections not hammered repoussé pieces.

All but one of the 1,799 armature bars were forged of *genuine puddled wrought iron* five-eights of a inch thick and two inches wide; one was copper. Their shapes followed the specific shapes of the statue. The front of one was fastened to the rear of another. Five-eighths of an inch diameter bolts and nuts fastened them to common splice plates. The bars ran in horizontal bands around the perimeter. Each level was set approximately four feet above the other. Every third section had bars that connected the horizontal bands to the structural steel pylons. The bars were fastened to the skin by flanged copper saddles. Bars required between three and eight saddles. Each saddle had six or eight rivets. Two and half million rivets were used to fasten all of Lady Liberty's joints.

Eiffel, knowledgeable about electromotive forces, knew that iron would sacrifice itself to preserve copper. Yet an interface between the two dissimilar materials was needed. The armature bars were painted with red lead. A paint like mixture of asbestos and shellac was applied to serve as an insulator to the surface of the bar that faced, but hopefully did not touch the copper skin. The system worked. There was only minor corrosion of iron and virtually no corrosion of copper. Copper pieces that failed, did so because the downward hammering had rendered them as thin as facial tissue.

This is not a criticism of the artisans. The fragility was a function of the point in time in which they were made. A hundred years later, with the same skills as our French forefathers, we were able to not repeat the errors of time. We incor-

*Craftsmen assemble pieces of the Statue's head*

porated late 20th century technology with timeless skills.

Bartholdi had given his mistress the title, *Liberty Enlightening The World*. Her first bout with Americanization came as her moniker was reduced to the *Statue of Liberty*. Once disassembled in France, her 214 crates were loaded on the French frigate *Isère*. The ship sailed through a storm that nearly capsized her. She arrived in New York in June of 1885, two months before construction of the pedestal.

Hunt's pedestal was the largest concrete pour in history at that time. General Charles P. Stone was the site engineer and clerk of the works.

The system to arrest lightning was implemented as the base of the pedestal was poured. A plate was set in the wet earth beneath the bottom of the foundation. Four, five-eighths of an inch round copper rods were extended downward from the base of the statue to attach to this plate. They were held in place as concrete was poured around them.

Similar copper bars were hammered to fit the interior surface of the skin. Like huge *Hula Hoops*, they were set apart randomly and were attached, via solder to the skin.

Historians are unsure who designed the system of anchorage. Two candidates are Eiffel and Stone. This system required two levels of structural steel set sixty feet apart. Sixty feet below, structural steel angles, plates and channels were set in the load bearing masonry walls. The base of the statue had a similar network of structural steel. Two levels were attached with structural steel *tie rods*.

Hundreds of workmen were billeted on Bedloe's Island for twenty months to build the pedestal. While they toiled a group of twenty-eight men moved on the island. They too were billeted. They unloaded the parts of the statue and laid them out in staging areas at the base of the pedestal.

The pedestal was turned over to the erection crews on April 22, 1886. Could they finish for a July 4th celebration?

No!

Rather amazingly, twenty-eight men erected the structural steel and copper skin in six months.

There were no unions.

Eiffel, ten years later, when he erected his famous tower, showed not only genius but cleverness. He trained circus acrobats to set the structural steel and were taught to throw, catch and set hot rivets. They worked a thousand feet in the sky and one man was killed. He died because he showed off for a girl friend after the work day had ended.

What tricks had been up Eiffel's sleeve for Lady Liberty? Did he already have a similar plan in mind for the Statue of Liberty? He never came to America, but did he write to Stone about it? We will never know. But we do know that they used no major scaffolding. A crane, perhaps steam powered, hoisted the structural steel pieces to ironworkers who climbed and vaulted to meet them. Once secured, bolts and nuts tightened and the rivets *bucked* the next pieces were set in place. Derricks were attached to the structural steel members of the head from which Bo'suns chairs were attached. Two and four man teams set the structural steel and copper skin. Inside the craftsmen climbed the iron infrastructure and perhaps used Bo'suns chairs. Outside they used the Bo'suns chairs.

Lady Liberty's right arm was misaligned. Experts disagreed upon the causes. One view was that copper skin was flattened during transit and required modifications. Another is that photographs taken in Paris showed the arm in a state of Bartholdi's redesign. Still another insists that Eiffel had become disinterested and did not care if Bartholdi changed the setting. A fourth is that the American crew simply made an error. Could not such misalignment be attributed to rigors of travel to and from Philadelphia years before? Rumors aside, the arm was set eighteen inches off to the side and slightly forward. Strong winds moved it three feet, depending upon the prevailing winds, into one of the spikes of the crown. An unpleasant piece of lore was born, it suggested that the errors of the arm created antipathy between Bartholdi and Eiffel. Like the arm, this blows in the wind.

In a fifty mile per hour wind, the statue only moves three inches. Anti-segregationist, Branch Rickey, baseball's most noted humanist would have said, "Eiffel's '...luck was the residue of good design?'"

One can only muse the life of these talented craftsmen. The spring, summer and fall weather allowed them to be comfortable with their out of doors billeting. What stories they must have told over the campfires. It is rumored that some of the workers took scraps of copper and made urns and trinkets in their spare time. The value of the pieces was vested in the historical value of the copper.

The statue was dedicated with great fanfare on October 28, 1886. Though cold, rainy and windy thousands upon thousands participated. Women, however, were excluded. They were angry! Suffragettes rented a large boat and sailed to the island. They shouted their complaints through megaphones and caused great confusion on the island.

Bartholdi, in a tuxedo, ascended, presumedly via a network of ladders, to the head and draped a Tricolored flag across her face. He waited for a bugler to blow a particular note to signal the moment of unveiling. Folklore is mixed here. One story said that the suffragettes caused chaos and the bugler sounded his note to alert security.

Another story played upon the supposed antipathy between Bartholdi and Eiffel. The rumor said that a friend of Eiffel's tipped the bugler five dollars to sound the note when alerted. One thing was clear, the note was sounded three hours early.

The euphoria of the moment forgave all sins. The Statue of Liberty was alive and well in New York Harbor.

Erected in the early stages of the patinization process, she had the rich chocolate color of statuary bronze. The migration toward her final verdigris was in progress.

One early sketch showed a spiral stair in her core. Yet none is known to have been made. An ingenious double deck helix, one to go up, one to come down, was made, two years after Bartholdi's death, by the Brooklyn Iron Works in 1906.

Lady Liberty sat quietly in the harbor serving as a lighthouse until 1902. In 1913 sculptor Gutzon Borglum, later to attain fame with Mount Rushmore tried to enhance the illumination. He cut six hundred openings in the torch and replaced the missing pieces with glass. Once modified, the torch leaked severely from rainwater and snow melt.

Maintenance staff literally punched holes in the copper to expel water than had congregated.

World War I German saboteurs set fires to the Black Tom munitions depot in Jersey City. Fragments from the explosion lodged themselves in the skirt and torch of the statue. The explosion registered a 5.5 on the Richter Scale. Damages were extensive. The cost of the repair was $100,000. The torch was closed to the public and has, appropriately, remained closed to this day.

*Gennaro "Bruno" Ranieri*

# Chapter 22
# A Framework For Restoration

I met John Robbins, Historical Architect for the National Park Service at the Theodore Roosevelt Birthplace Museum on East Twentieth Street, Manhattan in 1981. A slender, gracious, good looking man, he often wore a bow tie. He reeked of antebellum charm and dry wit. He was a little younger than I, but much smarter. We were chatting one day when he said, "I recommended you for work on the Restoration of the Statue of Liberty. You'll probably be getting a phone call soon." I smiled, thanked him and hoped that he didn't see my heart beating through the jacket of my suit.

I was perplexed. If we were not involved with the Statue, clients might think that we weren't good enough. If we got involved we might not be able to

*Ranieri forging new armature bar for the nose*

141

service them. Was it too big for me? I had often been accused of being ethereal, never wanting real "contracts", never being a "business man." Business was good the way it was, a nine man shop was perfect. We always had work. The men knew that had job security, fifty-two weeks a year, every year. Our major flaw was that we were often late completing work. It may have taken longer, but as some clients said, "It was worth the wait." This would be a new world.

I talked it over with Dick Hanington. He suggested that I talk to the museums before I made up my mind. I did and received their blessings.

A few days later Hanington helped me formulate a plan. He said, "Don't let the Statue burn Bruno out. Let him be the teacher." Hanington knew that Bruno could wear many hats. Yet we worried about his ability to teach. Ranieri taught by example. He said "watch me," and assumed that if you watched, you could do it. Sometimes it worked.

Hanington and I were playing golf one day when he stopped short and said, "Joey, I don't want to hurt your feelings, but you don't have the 'high rise' mentality. You care about the work; they only care about the money. You're okay when it comes to writing proposals and writing change orders, but I don't think that you can negotiate with these guys. These guys can chew you up and spit you out."

"What do you suggest?"

"Maybe we can find a real project manager for you. You run the work, let him be strong arm guy, You sure can't be."

*Micro blasting an armature bar to remove red lead paint and asbestos*

142

"Good idea. Are you going to putt that ball or not?" He stroked the ball into the hole and smiled.

I asked Robbins about this. He was quiet at first, then with hesitation he said. "Joe, they know this. They're in a peculiar position. They're afraid to do it with you and their afraid to do it without you. They'll have a plan. Relax."

Robbins, Lawrence Bellante, and Ziva Benderly visited the shop on August 4, 1983. They brought an armature bar and piece of 316L Stainless Steel.

Bellante was the "B" in the esteemed engineering firm of GSGSB. An energetic man of average height he was gracious, witty, and smart. Benderly, Associate Director of Restoration and Preservation, was everybody's lovable Rubenesque mother. She had worked hard to show her mettle and was rewarded. She proved that women were indeed equal to men and she proved it with grace.

As was customary, we offered coffee to everyone and I introduced Ranieri. He sported a huge smile and friendly handshake and told everyone, "Call me Bruno."

They were curious to see the jobs in progress and were pleased when they saw the copper being worked for the Semans job and iron being forged for a decorative door for a client in Houston.

They wanted to know everything. More coffee was in order.

Bellante looked at Bruno and said, "Can you copy this?"

Reverting to his native Italian, he said, "*Naturalmente.*"

Fractured English not withstanding he was an ambassador. He looked at the convoluted bar of *genuine puddled wrought iron*, and said, "Do you want to watch how we do this?"

Leonard Bernstein could not have orchestrated it any better. In unison they smiled and said, "Yes, please."

"Follow me, but watch your step," he said.

Joe Karhut joined him at the forge, added more coal, pushed the electric bellows to high and placed the stainless bar in the firebox. The group waited in quiet anticipation, as the bar started to turn red, then redder, then yellow and finally white, *snowball* white, sputtering sparks. Ranieri and Karhut had made the original into a template and had mounted it into a large leg vise. They extracted the work piece with tongs and set it on top of the template. Then, using long forks, which we always called by the German name, *gabels*, they pulled and coaxed the hot bar to fit its master. Once in place, the piece was hammered to fit its mate. Cooled, it was returned to the fire and the process was repeated. Luckily, it was a short bar and only a few heats were necessary.

We didn't have enough time to let it air cool, Ranieri thrust the still hot bar into a tank of water. A loud hiss and a curtain of steam rose. After a minute of bathing, it emerged cool enough to touch.

Ranier and Karhut were sweating; this was hard work and everyone saw it. Bellante and Robbins had been very close to the work and were somewhat dirtied. They didn't care as they smiled,

Bellante asked, "Can you finish it off?" Ranieri got the gist and took a center punch and dimpled spots for a few holes. He gave the bar to Giacomo Novielli and told him to drill two holes for tapping (threading) a half inch diameter bolt and two holes to be *slip holes*. We had a magic drilling machine that had six drill heads. One machine that did the work of six. Novielli went through the five required phases in about a minute and half.

Smiling, Bellante asked, "Can you weld it?"

"Let's find out," I said.

Ranieri was already searching for stainless steel welding rods. He looked at me and nodded.

We read each others minds, "weld to what?" He put the bar into the band saw and cut off a few inches. He gave both pieces to Tony DelVecchio, "Tony," he said, "weld these." DelVecchio ground *V's* into the mating surfaces, lined up the pieces, and welded them.

Bellante had taken an extra welding shield and watched.

DelVecchio asked "Do you want me to finish it?" I nodded.

He ground and sparks flew. Finished, he put the bar in a vise and filed the joint clean.

Robbins asked, "What kind of finishes can we have?"

"I don't know, let's find out."

Walter Gonzalez took the bar and applied greaseless compound to a polishing wheel and produced a mild satin finish. Everyone looked at it, but hanging in the air was, "What else?"

Benderly asked, "What would a blasted finish look like?" Gonzalez took the bar to the sandblasting room, put on his air fed helmet, stoked the pressure pot with blasting media, turned on the dust collection system and closed the doors. Loud hissing noises emanated from the chamber. The group, peered through a window in the metal wall and watched as a mini tornado blasted a textured, uniform finish.

Bellante asked, "If you have suggestions of another way to do this, tell us?"

"Can I keep the bar?" I asked, referring to the original that we had just copied.

The bar, though it had been covered with paint, asbestos and rust appeared to be in great shape after micro-blasting. Five-eighths of an thick by two inches wide is very substantial. Some areas showed minor pitting as a function of the rust, but nothing appreciable.

"Mr. Bellante," I said.

"Call me Larry."

"Larry, what's wrong with it?" He smiled sheepishly and shrugged.

" Can I have some friends look at it? One's a preservationist at the Metropolitan Museum, the other's a metallurgist/scientist."

"Sure," he said.

Much later, firmly entrenched in processes, we discovered that of the 1,799 bars, one was made of copper. Only five of the original genuine puddled wrought iron bars had deteriorated enough to warrant replacement.

Ranieri, Karhut, DelVecchio, Eddie Assas and I gathered around the coffee pot. Karhut asked, "Isn't this *puddled iron*? It don't rust."

Ranieri explained, "When I was a boy we used to put wax on it when it was hot, it never rusted."

"What are you going to do, Joe?" Asked Assas.

"I'm gonna talk to Steve and Richie." They all knew and liked both of them.

I called Smith and Weintraub.

We met the next day at Smith's lab with the *genuine puddled wrought iron bar*. I related Bellante's request.

We studied the bar with magnifiers. Smith took a small slice and put it under a microscope. You could see that the bar had been too short at one time, Gaget in order to save material, fire welded two pieces to make one. The weld was perfectly intact, and showed itself with only a slight line.

"How many are there? Smith asked.

"Eighteen hundred, plus or minus."

"Can we see them?"

I called Bellante's office and asked if we could go out to the statue. He made arrangements and we boarded the National Park Service (NPS) launch at Battery Park. Once inside the statue both Smith and Weintraub understood all of the forces at work. The statue is approximately forty feet wide at the base. Beams of sunlight entered through holes in the skin where rivets used to be. Wind whispered and the lady's skirts were ruffled. A curious noisy quiet. This lady had a personality. We felt her welcoming us.

Smith said "Is this fresh air or chloride (salt) air, Steve?"

"Both I think. Depends which way the wind blows. The river is here, the ocean is there," he said as he crossed his arms pointing in different directions.

I hadn't connected the dots yet. Smith knew it. He said, "some guys think that the metals' nobilities behave differently in salt air."

"Meaning?"

"In salt air, the electromotive force potential (EMF) may cause the copper to react more severely with iron."

Weintraub said, "Do you think that's what happened here?"

"The copper looks fine. I doubt it."

"How much time do we have to prepare a study?" Smith asked.

"How much do you need?

"A couple of days."

"I'm sure that will be fine."

Finished inside we decided to study her from outside. We climbed on the freshly erected scaffolding to her nose. We stood there wondering how much corrosion there may be on the outside.

147

Weintraub said, "Conventional wisdom is that acid rain is overrated. Some scientists think that its only the first ten seconds and then it gets washed off."

We noticed that the left side of her face was a darker color than her right. Why?

We all felt the abrasive particles that were blowing in the wind. We should have worn goggles. I asked Smith, "Is this a mild form of micro-blasting?"

"Maybe you're right, its just so mild, like Pumice or Rottenstone powder, that it keeps it clean."

This was to be observed and studied in detail. No absolute determination was ever agreed upon.

Smith and Weintraub once again put on their genius hats and came up with a plan. They decided that fresh air or chloride didn't matter. They proposed to bathe the original bars in a mild solution to loosen the paint and shellac laced asbestos. The residue would be removed with micro-blasting with walnut shells.

Here Smith took over. Each bar would be plated with a *tin-nickel* alloy and four strikes (coats) of copper. Galvanic action would be virtually obviated. Copper to copper surfaces would be in equilibrium. The *coup de grâce* was an inter-layer of *Indium*.

I interrupted Smith to interject that DuPont had donated Teflon tape to be the interface agent. Smith just smiled, "Good, I was going to get to that."

Unperturbed by my rudeness he said, "*Indium* is an oxygen scavenger. On any humid day it will absorb the moisture from the air and spit it back out on a dry day. The bars will never, ever rust!"

"The bars may be work hard from fighting the wind and sun for a hundred years. They can be heat treated to anneal them. They'll be better than new."

They wrote an extensive report. Bellante fascinated, visited with Smith.

Smith told me, "I think I made a believer of him. He wanted to know how much it would cost."

The Statue of Liberty/Ellis Island Foundation had already received a gift of fifty thousand pounds of 316L stainless steel and Ferrulum bars from an American association of stainless steel manufactures. Metallurgists for the Foundation had chosen low hydrogen stainless steel, the "L," because its electromotive potential was similar to that of copper.

The association planned to fully advertise the benefits of stainless steel. A year and half later we were called upon to substantiate the value of their "charitable contribution." The materials when purchased in small quantities sold for ten dollars a pound. When sold in quantities as large as fifty-thousand pounds the cost per pound plummeted to one dollar.

Smith and Weintraub had indeed raised many eyebrows.

Bellante called to thank them for their "tantalizing scheme." The Foundation weighed the options. Great similarities in both schemes allowed them to comfortably stay with 316L stainless steel. Smith, not comfortable, offered a suggestion to lessen the odds. His report is printed as an appendix to this chapter.

Some time passed as the Foundation was assembling their team. Lehrer/McGovern, Inc. was awarded the contract for construction management.

Eugene McGovern, called Gene by everyone, scheduled an off hours visit to our shop. His intent was to see the shop while it slept and interview me. A large bald man seemingly always sporting a cigar, he emitted the image of a tough guy. He was, but when and if he smiled he was a nice guy with a nice sense of humor. He came with a group of four and toured the floors of the shops. As a New York City facility we had grown into adjacent buildings and all the floors as we needed them. They toured the different shops, inspected the works in progress, and wore poker faces.

I said to myself, "Self, don't these guys ever smile?" Finished in the shops they came upstairs to the office. McGovern, still in his tough guy role, asked questions not about our work, but about my business skills or rather lack of them. He said, "No handshakes here. Can you handle contracts?"

I used one of my favorite lines, "I'm no pair of empty shoes."

He blinked, smiled and softened, then changed the subject and talked about golf. The interview was over.

McGovern had appointed Phillip Kleiner as their project manager. He called and asked that I take him to some of our jobs that were in progress. A mid fifties, bespectacled, slightly balding man of average build, he, at first wore the company issue, tough guy suit. Once again I mumbled to myself, "What's wrong with these guys?" I wouldn't want to play poker with any of this group.

I showed him the ongoing restoration of the Semans' house across from the Metropolitan Museum. He studied everything and said little, then we went across the street to the American Wing. He looked at the Sullivan Stair as if it were a fire stair in a warehouse. I was in tough company.

Hanington and I had breakfast as we usually did the next day and, he laughed so hard, he cried, "Joey, I told you."

Requests For Proposals were sent by Lehrer/McGovern to ironworks all over the world. "Proposal" was a misnomer, it was a "bid." The "bid package" included bid bonds, performance bonds and completion bonds.

When Hanington and I had collaborated to restore Bow Bridge, architect Geoffrey Platt asked if we thought that the City should require surety protection. Hanington somewhat surprised, said to Platt, "No, why not get life insurance on Joe?" Platt had smiled and the issue was never raised again.

We procured the bonds and tendered our "bid". I was called to a meeting of members of the Foundation as well as Lehrer/McGovern. I was comfortable seeing the friendly faces from the members of Foundation and the National Park Service. McGovern's staff always played poker. So be it. When the meeting ended, I was led to a back door for exit. The message was clear, competitors were waiting their turns in the outer office.

A few days later I was asked to come to a meeting at McGovern's office and to "bring an open mind." McGovern came up to me while I waited in the anteroom. I rose, he smiled and put an arm around my shoulder as he led me to the conference room. He said what Robbins had said earlier, "Joe, they're afraid to do it with you, but they're more afraid to do it without you."

I sat around a large glass conference table with McGovern and Kleiner.

McGovern commanded the floor, "We want to marry you to someone. A big company. We figure we'll get the best of both worlds." He searched my face, but I had taken a page from their book. My face was blank.

He continued, "If you don't like this company, we'll get you another one, we have three in mind."

I was a little scared who my mail order bride was, but I was relieved. I could focus on the work. I smiled and said, "Okay."

The meeting ended and Kleiner said, "I want you to meet someone. Hang around for a while."

I borrowed a desk, made some phone calls, had a cup of coffee and waited.

Kleiner took me to another glass walled conference room. As we entered, a man was sitting with his back to me. He didn't turn, didn't get up, didn't acknowledge me. "Here we go again," I thought. I went around the table to face Edward Simpson. He fit the mold of the day, mid fifties, receding hairline, spectacled and detached if not rude.

Kleiner with an attempt at humor, said, "I'm the rabbi, I pronounce your man and wife."

Simpson didn't blink, just extended his hand across the table. His eyes never met mine. Kleiner and I sat down. Kleiner read the amounts of both "bids." Ours was three million, five hundred thousand dollars. Nab Construction, Inc., one of Simpson's companies was three million, three hundred thousand dollars.

Simpson said to Kleiner, "We'll use our price." Wow, and I'm not a good business man?

I asked Kleiner if we could caucus for a minute, he left the room, smiling.

"Mr. Simpson," I said.

"Call me Ed."

"Ed, they want us, we don't have to give anything away yet."

"Nah, you're too high. My man said it only takes two hours to make each bar."

"Ed, we've made a few of them. Soup to nuts, fifteen to twenty man hours, per bar."

"We'll show you how to do it faster."

"Joe," he said out of the corner of his mouth, "I'll cover any losses."

Kleiner reentered the room and we agreed.

I had taken a cab to McGovern's office on Park Avenue South. Simpson offered to drive me back to the shop. As we drove he softened a bit. The shop made him wax nostalgic about his early years and a humble facility such as ours.

It was a Friday and the day was waning. He said, "Can you meet me tomorrow?"

"I'm playing in a golf tournament."

"In the afternoon, anytime. Call me when you're finished. Come to my tennis club in Manhasset" (Long Island).

I met him and his wife at three o'clock the next day. I was happily surprised to see his gracious side. "I don't play golf," he said. "Takes too much time. We like tennis."

We had a bite to eat and he said, "we'll call it 'NAB/Fiebiger.'" Was that a play on words? He continued, "like I said before, I'll cover any losses."

We talked about unions. Some men, he agreed possessed special skills, but he snarled, as if angry, "A man's a man, they're all the same. When one guy can't do, just get another one."

Shocked, I softly muttered to no one. "Be still my lunch."

As I reflected driving home, somewhere in a fumbled way of the conversation he had very subtly let it slip that he would give me a hundred thousand dollars to "disappear." I noticed the look that his wife shot him as he gently backed away from it. Maybe it was my imagination, maybe not.

We agreed that I come to his office in College Point to meet his staff.

Monday morning I met Milton Einbinder and Joe Minetti. Einbinder fit the mid-fifties profile again, this time with pleasant twists. He too was bespectacled, but he had a full head of hair and beard. Better yet, he smiled, laughed, and looked the university professor. Sometimes he sounded like one. It was always comforting.

Minetti was stocky, mid thirties and jovial. He was the record keeper.

The three of us chatted, Einbinder explained life at NAB. He asked, "How many man hours did you figure per bar?"

"Fifteen to twenty."

Einbinder choked. Gil Schiller, a long time NAB employee had been assigned to be the field superintendant

Minetti said, "Gil, poked his head into Ed's office and said, 'don't worry boss, it only takes two hours for each bar.'"

"Did he make one?" I asked.

Einbinder just smiled, "No"

Einbinder was a pragmatist. He understood the "high rise" world and how it was affected by unions. He told me that no matter what anyone thought of Simpson, his strong suit was in dealing with unions.

We had been a union shop since the mid-fifties. Opa and Dad had installed work at Stark's Restaurant. Ironworker's Local 455 protested. Opa, an adamant opponent fought vigorously, but lost.

Dad had related the story in its full context. He said that there was blatant abuse in the industry. Wages were low, conditions dangerous, holiday pay and welfare were non-existent. The workers were abused. Opa and Dad ascribed to none of that; they felt that their family like relationships with the men was best. The union labor pool could not provide men with the talents that we needed. New men arrived when they were recommended by an employee.

That proverbial pendulum of labor and management was in motion. When and where the piper would be paid, no one knew. Still, Dad and Opa knew that a talented and productive labor force had to be treated with respect and dignity and applied their own standards.

Ironworks Local 455's was a Shopmen's union, termed an "inside" union. Its members worked in fabricating shops. Two other unions, deemed "outside unions," installed the fabricated work. William Colovito was the President of 455. He ran the union with the right intentions, but had an adversarial attitude that angered many. We had been under his radar. He and his executive board called us a "country club" to their rank and file. Colovito was supposed to have said, "I don't care if there's only one ironworker left in the city, he'll be the highest paid." The lines of antipathy and distrust were born and never quenched.

Our belief was that we did better work than most, certainly had a great clientele and basically never were called upon to compete. We paid higher wages and certainly didn't need a union to tell us that it was right to pay a man for his bereavement when mourning the death of a family member. We kept the coffee pot, with no designated "coffee break," because it was the right thing to do. Also, it was good business, an *esprit de corps* was engendered: the men talked about sports, usually soccer; politics; and sometimes work. They never talked sex.

The NAB's of the world had a way to get around 455. They hired ironworkers from the two outside unions. Local 40 and Local 580 were unions whose members installed the work that was made in shops.

Colovito had made the cost of doing business in New York City so high that many of the fabrication shops moved past the fifty mile radius that defined 455's territory. Colovito had not made friends with Locals 40 and 580. Had they declined to erect work made outside the city, 455 would have been strong. They declined. As a result, the rank and file membership of 455 dwindled from 4,000 to 400 in a relatively short period of time.

Einbinder described Colovito as "...a toothache that won't go away. ..." A few years later when Colovito drove his fangs into me, I likened it to "root canal."

The Foundation was planning to erect a pre-engineered building on Liberty Island to serve as a workshop. We planned to run two shops, one there and one at our Tenth Avenue facility. Einbinder managed to hammer out an agreement with Colovito to allow 580 to work in the Liberty Island shop along with 455 members. There was a modicum of peace.

However, no provisions were made for the arrival of Sheet Metal Worker's Local 28 when they "claimed" a portion of the work. Their skills would certainly be needed for the Ellis Island copper roof work. They had picked up the nickname, "Tin Knockers" for a reason and did not possess the skills required on the Statue. Their skills were needed on Ellis Island and they thrived there.

Einbinder wanted to introduce a talented craftsmen, Guisippe Micheli into our work force. Micheli, a member of 455, was forty-five, of modest size with a huge mustache. He was a friendly guy. He and Ranieri quickly earned each others respect. Micheli swallowed his ego for a while and deferred to Ranieri's superior talent.

Another amazing feat of engineering had happened at the Statue. Alan Shalders, an engineer with Universal Building Supply, Inc. designed a freestanding aluminum scaffolding system. It required no support from the Statue and never touched her. Every area of the exterior was accessible for relatively safe work.

We made a field trip to the Statue. Einbinder, Ranieri, Micheli, Karhut, Assas and I. El Hadi Assas was a French speaking Algerian. We called him Eddie. At the Statue I was introduced to Victor Callirgos and Peter B. Kaplan.

Another mid-fifties profile was filled by Callirgos. He was slight of build, blue eyed, with plenty of neatly combed grey hair. He wore glasses and exuded charm. As I reflected, I often thought that three most important players in saving Miss Liberty were Robbins, Ranieri and Callirgos. The role of draftsmen that was applied to Callirgos was a misnomer. He proved an old adage to which I had ascribed, "drawing is easy, thinking what to draw is hard." He figured out every facet of each piece of everything.

He never complained, as did I, when someone criticized one of my designs. I always asked the critic, "Where were you when the paper was blank?" He

*Annealing an armature bar*
*Left to Right: Joseph Fiebiger, Joseph Karhut and Gussipe Michieli*

and his staff were amazingly talented and were not petty.

We had entered the computer era in 1979. By 1983 we had evolved to a Unix operating system. We had accounting, job costing, word processing and spread sheet routines.

A visitor appeared and introduced himself as John McCloud. He represented an upstart Computer Aided Design (CAD) software company, AudoCad. He had learned of us when he read engineering magazines. I told him that Callirgos was the design arm of our venture. He offered to give us software and lend us three machines so that Callirgos could take the software for a test drive.

One of Callirgos' draftsmen, Danny Marro, had worked on an embryonic CAD routine at a different job. He said that they were still "too new." Callirgos offered to try it, but made no guarantees.

McCloud seemed pleased, gave us the programs and computers and only asked, that if we used them and they worked well, that we would give AutoCad credit. That was the extent of my authority. Marro was right, it was "too new."

157

Peter B. Kaplan was a good looking, forty-five year old man who extracted seventy minutes out of every hour. He and his assistants took pictures, pictures, then more pictures. He was devoted to being the accurate chronicler of the event. He was!

We were all standing in the large landing area where the statue and pedestal meet. It was raining outside and though dimly lit, we saw rivulets of water running down the copper skin. We felt her shudder in the wind, heard rattles, and listened to the wind whistle through holes left open from missing rivets. She was having a bad hair day, but she still welcomed us.

A love affair was born. Ranieri and Assas began to remove an armature bar. Assas passed a grinder over it and the metal screeched. Ranieri stopped Assas by touching his arm, "Careful, don't hurt her." The theme was set.

As Callirgos, Einbinder and I watched, we talked. I told them about Oscillation 101. How the Office of the Architect of the Capitol gave the course. Robert Landsman, an architect in the office Swanke, Hayden and Connell along with Robbins and Bellante had specified that the areas in which bars were removed had to be from four diametrically opposed points on the compass and be three tiers, approximately twelve feet part.

We enhanced it. We wondered if they had related this to anything other than wind loads, but that was academic. Our silent solution was to reinstall each bar at the same time of day that it had been taken out. The placement of saddles was moderately forgiving.

Callirgos established a numbering system for each bar as he drafted. Time of extraction was simple matter.

Simpson, determined to prove that a new bar could be copied in less than fifteen to twenty man hours, asked Einbinder and me to explore other possibilities.

I contacted manufactures of bending equipment and invited them to the shop to advise us. One company had recently invented a machine that bent automotive tail pipes. Their representative studied the bars and said that they would love to be involved. He was positive that they could make a machine that would first trace the existing bar and then, with operators present, bend the bars. The machine could not however make twists. The procedure had to be interrupted when the machine hit a twist. Then the bar would be heated and twisted with the *gables*. The machine would then finish the task.

This could appreciably reduce the amount of very arduous labor that were required. The company wanted the rights to advertise their completed product and three hundred thousand dollars. The money would only be paid when and if the machine worked.

I was optimistic, Einbinder was skeptical and Simpson went ballistic. That dead, I called the well known German machinery manufacturer, Peddinghaus. They made a variety of machines for bending and cutting metals. They had a machine for bending heavy concrete reinforcing bars, *rebar*. Simpson thought the machine would work. I saw the problem with the twists. The machine could not produce them.

We bought it and had it shipped via air freight from Germany for twenty-five thousand dollars. It didn't work and almost severed my hand as I watched Karhut and Assas use it. Accidents are just that, accidents. I had been watching and had said to Karhut, "Wait, wait!" He didn't hear me, hit the button and down came the iron bar.

A hundred and forty-five stitches later, I was a very lucky guy.

The day after the stitches were removed, with a guarded blessing from my doctor, I played in golf a tournament. My hand was so tender that I had to swing easily. I won the tournament.

This is fully explained in chapter fifteen of *Go Figure*.

Callirgos had finished his drawings, all bars were identified and we began the replacement process.

We tried to take negative impressions of the existing bars in a variety of ways. Plaster casts that were used in emergency rooms and podiatrist's foam didn't work. We couldn't use the existing bar, its five-eights of inch thickness made our reproductions off by that thickness. Ranieri knew, he chose to hammer flat iron bars, one eighth of an inch thick by two inches wide to mimic the original bars. This was a task that was easy for one as talented as he, but others worked hard to learn. Once formed, each was fastened to a base plate with welded struts. There was ample room above and below to allow the *gables* to fit, and they were strong enough to allow furious hammering while they took the heat.

Simple bars, and there were some, were formed cold using the power of our one hundred ton, triple action hydraulic press. New copper saddles were also formed with the press.

Einbinder, advised Simpson of the prognosis. "Ed wants to find an easier way." We both laughed. Fifteen to twenty hours it would be. What was the problem, my budget had been predicated on that number.

Simpson's gracious offer to "cover any losses," had put me back in an environment in which I thrived. The success of the work was my master. Ironic, a man whose personality was unable to combine power and grace as our patrons did, was in fact a patron of sorts.

Once, in frustration he yelled at me, "You're the damned conscience of Statue." I said nothing. He continued, "I guess I always knew that." The walls had ears. I heard that again and again. Actually, I grew to like it.

Ranieri and I shared an audio talent. We could tap a piece of metal, me with my ring, he with a hammer, and determine what kind of metal it was. Each metal has its own tone, as does its hardness. Berra said, "You can see a lot by watching." Well, Yogi, you can hear at lot by listening, too.

We had just started reproducing the bars. The techniques worked well. As the bars were worked, the sounds, though loud, were pleasing.

Have you ever reflected on the worst sounds that you ever heard? There were two, the second came a few years later when our first Apple computer crashed and emitted its horrible death tone. The first, worse than fingernails across a chalkboard, was the tone of a completed stainless steel armature bar.

I heard an alien noise drift up through the ceiling of the shop into the office. Immediately I heard, "Joe." I scampered down the spiral stair and saw Ranieri holding the bar, his face fraught with disbelieve.

"Its too hard," he said. He tapped it again, I came over and tapped it with my ring. "Don't drop it on the floor," he said jokingly, "it'll break."

The bar, six feet long was shaped like a Chinese noodle. Heated, cooled, levered into place and hammered to fit, All those processes had rendered it *work hard*.

Ranieri and DelVecchio took to two large oxygen-acetylene torches, set them to high and passed them over the bar until it turned, yellow. We would have needed four torches to get them to white hot. Yellow and cooling, DelVecchio took it outside. Gonzalez brought a garden hose. It hissed and water boiled on its surface, steam rose as he sprayed it. Wet and cool, Ranieri gave it his tone test. The sound was pleasant. My ring agreed.

We knew what we had to do, but how to do it 1,798 (the original copper bar was to be reused) times was another matter.

*The completed new stainless seel armature network*

Everyone was surprised at this hiccup. We all thought that the immense amount of heat required for the bending would be its own annealing vehicle. The stainless steel manufactures said that they didn't foresee this. Bellante was smart, and passed no blame. He just wanted a solution.

Ed Onny of LORS machinery jumped into my mind. He was a bold and innovative thinker. I hoped that he would remember me from the Gainesway Farm job. I called him and unfolded the story. "Can you create a huge short circuit?" I asked.

"Let me think about it for a while?" The phone went silent for moment. "Okay, I've got it. It'll be a controlled short circuit. We'll jury-rig a resistance welder. It'll take a couple of days. It'll work."

Meanwhile, Bellante had received input from the stainless manufactures. They said that if the bars were heated to 1905 degrees Fahrenheit for two minutes and quenched in cold water, all properties would be restored.

Onny called, "I think we've got something that will work. Do you want to come and see it work."

"Should I see it first, or can the whole group come?"

"Bring all the people you have. It works!" He said with a rising voice.

Einbinder set the process in motion. Bellante, Kleiner, Benderly, Einbinder and I drove to New Jersey in two cars. We took a few completed bars.

Introductions were made, the usually calm and gracious Bellante was like a cat on a hot tin roof. Onny sensed it, took one of the bars and led us into his shop.

We stopped by an eight foot long, two foot wide apparatus. It was lined with fire bricks and had two large arms. They held very thick wires with immense clamps to hold the bar and transmit the electricity. Two water hoses delivered water to cool the heating devices. Under the machine was a large water tank that was filled with cold water

Onny placed a clamp on each end, set the bar steady with additional fire bricks and turned up the power. Bellante glanced at his watch. Onny said, "It'll take eight hundred amps. It'll work."

He painted the bar with a 2000 degree Fahrenheit *temperature stick* and started the flow of current. Slowly the bar turned red, then redder, yellow came next followed quickly by white. The stick, announced our arrival at the temperature. Onny set the rheostat and maintained the heat for two minutes. Then his assistants removed the clamps and picked the bar with tongs. As they dropped it in the tank, they, with us in unison, backed away to the see the steam and hear the hiss.

Cool now, the bar was removed from the tank to everyone's applause. I tapped it with my ring. It was the sound we wanted.

Onny cautioned, "You can't use those 'Tempil Sticks.' Get some *infrared pyrometers*."

He knew that we needed two of these machines, one for the shop on Liberty Island the other for our shop. He didn't yet know what they would cost, but he asked a favor.

"If we make these for you, can we put our company logo on them?" He asked.

"Of course," was Bellante's reply.

As we drove back to Manhattan I asked Einbinder, "Please don't let Ed embarrass me. Onny's an honest guy. Don't go shopping."

"I don't think Ed will do that. The Foundation's picked up the costs, plus an extra for the labor required. Don't worry."

Onny proposed to make the two machines for ninety-five thousand dollars. Einbinder was right, no one blinked. Onny had proven that business the old fashioned way still worked. He had gambled and lost a few years earlier, made a friend, and ultimately was rewarded. A nice story.

Electricians set up the machine on Liberty Island in short order. In our shop it was another matter. We did not have enough power in the building. Consolidated Edison would have to run new service from thirty-fourth street to thirty-sixth. Nonplused by the importance, their representative said that it would three months to get these power lines.

I called Kleiner and reported the events. The next day Con Ed crews ran the new wires. It took two days and was ready to be connected to the new electrical equipment that we had to have installed.

I called Kleiner again, this time to ask him how he had pulled this rabbit out of hat. "Simple, Lee (Iaocca) called Mr. Luce." Mr. Luce was the CEO of Con Ed.

The cost of the electrical equipment to run this machine was thirty-five thousand dollars. Simpson, charmingly ballistic, called and said, "I'm not paying for that! If the Foundation pays okay, otherwise you're on your own! You eat it! Its your building!"

I started to explain that if we had needed that much amperage before, we would have already had it. But by now, I knew better.

The issue was mute, the Foundation never questioned the electrician's charges.

We had established the routine to replicate the bars. Modern Hydraulics had manufactured two, fifty ton hydraulic presses. New employees arrived and were trained to make the bars, saddles and buck rivets.

We began a pilot project. A crew removed two bars from each designated section. Each three tiers above the other at opposed points on the compass. The time of day and weather were noted on the drawings. The *genuine puddled wrought iron* bars were micro-blasted, templates were formed and the new stainless steel bars, *fishplates* and saddles were made. We decided to drill to the holes in saddles while they were being installed, this allowed for minor and harmless deviations. The new bars were lightly blasted to remove the discolorations caused by the heat. A Teflon strip, backed with adhesive was applied to the interface.

Bellante and his extended staff had conquered a major dilemma. They had explored innumerable methods of removing the existing coats of paints on the interior surface of the copper skin. Layers of paint had been applied over the coal tar base that the National Park Service had applied many years past. They were removed by the brilliant discovery to use baking soda as a cleaning agent. The soda slipped through seams and holes and caused minor discolorations that we chemically repaired during the patinization phase.

Everyone knew that the statue was essentially a chimney. Fire precautions, at all times were paramount. Flash fires or explosions would have been catastrophic. How then to remove the coal tar? Any volatile compound was, naturally excluded. Blasting with anything other than an organic substance like walnut shells would remove too much good material while removing the paint. Voilà, liquid Nitrogen. Four hundred fifty nine degrees below zero Fahrenheit (-459) it created an immense thermal shock. The paint came off in pieces as large a potato chips. The task quickly completed, they faced another challenge.

We began the replacement procedure amid the blasting and chaos. Bars were installed. All appeared to be going well. But not for long. Another crisis was upon us. They had started to *bloom*, to rust.

Stainless steel is stainless because the *chromium oxides* on the surface protect it. These *oxides*, if removed expose the iron in steel. Naturally they pick up a *bloom.*

Once more, it was "All hands on deck." Bellante and his team were furious. Their first thought was that they had been given an inferior grade. The manufactures adamantly maintained that the materials donated were of prime quality. They said that stainless steel will become "cosmetically stained" in certain situations. One situation being when the material had undergone rigorous forming procedures. "Cosmetic" was the buzz word. They maintained that the structural

*Lowering of the Torch*
*July 4th, 1984*

properties had not been compromised. I heard that someone on the Foundation, it sounded likes Robbins' humor, said, "Pretty counts here, too."

Yet again, another mind boggling problem. Lady Liberty was throwing some major curves our way. Who better to eliminate a catastrophe than Richie Smith? He wasn't surprised when I called him for advice.

Smith understood various procedures for what is called *passivation*. Some procedures in fresh air environs, called for submersion of the of the parts into a bath of nitric acid. Smith was more concerned about the unknown relationships the fresh and chloride airs in which Lady Liberty sat. Fresh air he stated was our friend, chloride our enemy.

He joked when he said, "If they ever do rust, then we'll finally know about the air in the harbor."

He formulated a recipe and work procedure that passivated the bars and restored their "cosmetic beauty." He enhanced his recipe to forgive expo-

*Balinda and Paul*

168

sure to chloride air. If the bars were ever again to show a *bloom*. They would be "healed" *in situ*.

He had a relatively simple procedure. Smith and many other scientists believed carbon dioxide emitted from the visitors contributed to this blemish. His recipe was proprietary. He didn't patent it and he never revealed it. The forgiving features of Smith's recipe would be implemented with closure of the statue for three days while air generators (pumps) filled the statue with fresh air.

The logistics were staggering. One crew was at work during the normal work day on the island. Two shifts were run at our Manhattan shop. The second shift ended about ten o'clock. Smith had to have a crew to pickup, deliver and passivate so that the bars from each of three shifts were at the dock by seven the next morning.

He and Weintraub figured it all out. They prepared a proposal. I accompanied Smith to the meeting with Kleiner. I had witnessed Kleiner go from a scowling poker faced tough guy to a regular fellow. He had mellowed. Until today. We sat at a conference table intended for sixteen. Kleiner at one end, presumedly the head, Smith at the other end, me, naturally enough in the middle.

Kleiner had read Smith's proposal. Scientists for the Foundation had alerted him that Smith's plan would work. He knew it was the stuff of which geniuses are made. Yet he had on his tough guy face. He peered over his glasses down the long table, "You can't be serious, four hundred thousand dollars for this?"

Smith, wearing tie and jacket, looked out of place without a lab coat. He didn't blink. He started to explain the costs of chemicals, costs of labor and the overtime mandated for his crews.

Kleiner cut him off, "We've got somebody who will do it for free."

Smith, eyes downward, smiled slightly and started to put his papers in his briefcase. He hesitated for a moment, looked up and across the divide and said, "What you get free is worth nothing."

Kleiner took the punch gracefully. He smiled and said, "I'll get back to you."

Wow, I wouldn't want to play poker with Smith either.

Kleiner called Smith and they agreed to a schedule of payments.

The armature bar replacement work took on a personality of its own. Hard, gruelling, challenging work. The men were tired and proud. Narcissism had taken root. Reporters from magazines and newspapers, foreign and domestic flocked to interview men of different ethnicities. Micheli fell first victim, he told a newspaper in Rome that he was the most talented of all the men. Ranieri was his underling.

Ranieri, though his feelings were hurt was too dedicated to let his vanity get in the way. It got easier for him when another Italian newspaper set the record straight and his relatives in the Abruzzi region took pride. Micheli apologized, said he didn't really say it like that; we all believed him.

The Black and Decker Manufacturing Company was an accredited sponsor. They had donated hand tools with the right to advertise that their tools were the tools being used for the restoration.

Without our approval, they modified a percussion drill to be a rivet gun. We taught the men how to set copper rivets without mis-hittng and damaging the copper. A two man procedure. The man on the outside placed a rivet with a pre-patinated head in the holes in the skin and the saddle. He applied pressure to the head with a hammer that had been covered with cloth. The man inside made certain the saddle fit properly and then hammered the shaft of the rivet. It was a acquirable skill. Done properly it took between four and five strikes of the hammer.

The new toy had converted a simple mechanical task to the chaos. No longer rhythmic and pleasing, it now resembled an aircraft fabrication plant.

The inmates were running the asylum. Schiller, the supervisor was supposed be in charge. He clearly was not. Simpson had been overheard when he told Schiller "...Fiebiger is the damn conscience, we'll never make any money with him around. ..."

Robbins was horrified. Every rivet that was bucked using this new device left many little half circle impressions on the skin. Also, in order to gain leverage, the man on the outside had to support himself with his back against the scaffolding and his feet against the skin. Not only were there mis-hits, there were footprints.

Angry and determined to stop this, Robbins called for a meeting to be held high up on Lady Liberty's skirts. He

*Technicans prepare for negative impressions for the new nose*

insisted that Simpson be present.

It was another one of those idyllic days. Warm, sunny with gentle breezes teasing us while water crafts went about their harbor business, seemingly at play. A horn would toot, a fire boat would spray water. Always a memorable experience.

Robbins and I arrived first and chatted. Stresses were getting to everybody, he was not immune, yet he managed to keep his gracious composure. I said to him, "Watch, Simpson will be the last to arrive." Sure enough, everyone was in place, waiting for the emperor.

When he arrived, Robbins' demeanor changed dramatically. He reiterated the scenario about the new rivet guns being unacceptable, the blemishes irreversibly implanted were, he said, "Criminal." It had to stop. "I watched Joe teach a group of your new workers how to set those rivets, its child's play!" Robbins continued, "How did all these footprints get here?"

Simpson hadn't been alerted to this issue. Taken by surprise and much to his credit, he sat down on the scaffolding and assumed the posture a workman would have used. His feet did not fit the dirty footprints. The footprints came from taller men. Simpson's defenses were running rampant, he said, "These aren't from my men."

Robbins grabbed my shoulder, pulled me away and turned me around. He was furious but he was laughing. "Do you have tall men or short men?" He asked.

I got his drift. "Both."

"Your partner thinks that you only have short men." His face had turned red from laughing. Bellante had caught the essence and held order. Everyone knew that the footprints would wash away, but they were angry that the statue was scarred.

Schiller had stayed in the background. Simpson lashed out at him. Schiller's response, "It's two hundred feet up, who'll see it?"

The new group of workers still had their way. They used the Black and Decker tools and found a way to not inflict scars.

So this was the world of "high rise."

Combined, both shops had approximately fifty men employed, twenty-five from each union. Our core group of nine was faithful to whom they always had been. The new group discredited them. Though we spoke many tongues, "Mediocrity" was in no one's vocabulary.

I had told all the men that I would have every man's name engraved on a simple brass plaque. The plaque would be riveted to the last armature bar. Each of the men would receive a miniature version for personal memorabilia. Everybody would be included.

Surreptitiously, Local 580 members made their own signature statement. They chose a long bar and stamped each man's name with rudimentary hand stamps. Only Schiller and the 580 crew knew. The secret was uncovered in an article written in *Smithsonian Magazine*.

Everyone in the Foundation and National Park Service went nuts. Rather than pass blame around, Bellante, besieged with phone calls, had all reporters call me.

I explained to one and all that it was born from justifiable pride, but was inappropriate. "Boys will be boys." I said. Most reporters pushed further, "Who is paying to fix this?"

"We are."

"What's it worth?"

"If the engineers think that it's okay, we'll grind it smooth and refinish it. Then we'll put in back in. Probably about three thousand dollars."

"Are you going to reprimand the workers?"

I was glad these were all telephone interviews, no body language at work here. I said, "No."

I was simply referred to as a company spokesmen and the issue melted away. Engineers saw nothing wrong with my suggested remedy. The victim was the plaque that I had promised everyone. Robbins, still angry over the incident, said, "You had the right idea, but drop it."

I had always wanted to make the new torch and flame. I sometimes questioned my wisdom or lack thereof, of getting involved in the armature phase. I thought that we could do both. The Foundation certainly liked us. We had already solved some major problems; more were yet to come.

The Foundation had interviewed metal workers all over the world. They traveled to visit these companies. I had a feeling that we were losing our front runner status. That aside, the torch was to be removed on July 4, 1984 to signal the official beginning of the restoration project.

We were asked to disconnect the torch from the arm. Once on *tierra firma* we were to make a pedestal for the torch, copying the original. The torch was put on display for the January 1st, Rose Bowl Parade in California. Upon its return it was displayed in the museum at the base of the statue.

Ranieri, Karhut, Assas, Gonzalez and I went to reconnoiter. The torch had been closed for seventy-one years. The only person who climbed the fourteen inch wide ladder was DeLeo, self proclaimed "Keeper of the Flame."

We chose to enter from the scaffolding. We vaulted over the repoussé balustrade carefully. I opened the door to the interior of the torch and was greeted by a Cathedral.

There were Masonic Crosses, crucifixes, saints medallions, liturgical coins, inscribed Bible verses, dates and initials. Were these from Gaget's artisans? Were these blessings bestowed by the French artisans to Americans?

Kaplan was photographing when I blurted out, "Have you seen this?"

"Yeah, I saw it. It's Charlie DeLeo's stuff. He's a real religious guy. Its down on the chains too."

"Are you sure? I asked.

"Pretty sure? No. Very sure, yes!"

I was confused, some of the artifacts were plastic, others seemed to be ivory. I had other fish to fry and made a note to ask Robbins.

Ranieri had placed himself in a comfortable seated position directly in front of the torch's connection to the pedestal. Hundreds of rivets had to be removed without scarring. Like a surgeon, he took a center punch and dimpled the center of few rivets. Assas then came along with a small drill bit and drilled a pilot hole. Karhut finished off the hole, changing different drill sizes until he found the right one. Bingo, the hundred year old head popped off and the body of the rivet was gently removed with a small punch.

Caught up in the actives of the event I had failed to notice the arrival of Robbins and Einbinder. Robbins observed the "unriveting," and was pleased. Einbinder had gone inside to study the structural steel that had to be cut.

NAB was now wearing two hats. They had been awarded the contract for the structural steel repairs. We disconnected the copper joints. Then their structural steel ironworkers disconnected the structural steel.

Early in the morning on the Fourth of July, Ranieri, Einbinder and I took scaffolding system's elevator to the torch. The weather was forecast to be hot with chances of thunderstorms. Members of every union on the job were there to take part. No bugler today. Everyone waited for a command via walkie talky.

We waited and watched the crowd of thirty-five thousand enter. Among them were Balinda, Beth, Paul and my proud mother. The walkie talkie barked a command and the event was in motion. All attention was on the torch as the crane began to lower it to the ground.

We began to place the plastic tarpaulin around the opening left by the torch. A section of soft carpet was set to the copper to prevent marring and the tarp was fastened. We were almost done when the sky turned black, the wind picked up and lightning was in the distance. We read each other's minds, "Hurry up." We hurried, but the rain started. Wet, cold, but safe, we took the elevator down.

No sooner had it started, it stopped and the sun came back out. The crowd had sought shelter. Paul had gotten lost in the melee. Balinda told a National Park Service Ranger that she was worried about me being up in the lightning and begged them to help find Paul. The walkie talkies proved useful, lost in a sea of legs, he

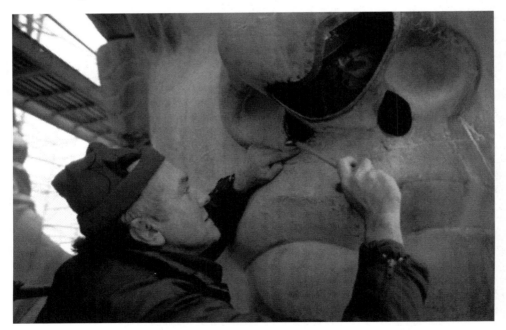

*Peter B. Kaplan in front of the lens, inspects the areas of the nose*

was safe.

We warmed in the sun and completed the day. Paul, atop my shoulders, waving an American flag had his picture on the front page of the *Daily News* the next day.

The Foundation traveled to Reims, France to visit the atelier of Les Métalliers Champenois (LMC). Jean Bourly their principal had visited our shop when he came to America. I invited him to my home and to dinner. We had discussed a possible venture. That, most certainly, was not to be.

They were awarded the commission to replicate the torch. I was disappointed. My disappointment didn't last too long. Gene McGovern sought me out on Liberty Island. He took me out of ear shot and said, "We know you're disappointed. This is political, it came from the White House. I've been told to tell you, and keep this to yourself, keep your mouth shut, just keep doing good work and you'll get Ellis Island."

I nodded, said, "Thanks." He was gone.

A group of about twelve young men came from France. Their leader, Jean Wiart was diminutive guy with vast amounts of energy.

Privately, I was envious of them. They had young, talented men. They had no union problems. I didn't think that they had anyone as good as Ranieri, but they came close. Both Ranieri and I disliked their constant self aggrandizement. They were not the only people on the planet who did repoussé work.

Ranieri and the other talented men respected the Frenchmen and their skills. Comically, the new group of men, much less talented and owing allegiance only to the union, were denigrating the French crew, saying that they could do the same work. Ranieri, Karhut, Assas, Micheli and DelVecchio could. They could not!

Ranieri, Micheli and Karhut did a delicate balancing act. They too were union members, but members of a different era and had a different ethic. They managed to care about the company and be union members. They often tried to protect me from myself.

I had been admonished because I criticized our shop steward severely. Anthony Rosaci was a union first personality. He cared little about anything else. He and the new group preached the unpardonable mantra to Ranieri, " Slow down, you're making us look bad."

I was angry when another of his mistakes was brought to my attention. A mistake, or sabotage? Stupid or lazy? I sarcastically said to him, "Imagine? Having to think and work, all in the same lifetime?" The quip was heard by many. He cited his em-

*Corroded curl*

barrassment as harassment and another unpleasant union event was in full swing.

One day Wiart was in trouble as he tried to convince Bellante of something. He said to Bellante, "Call Joe over here. He knows." I went over, listened to their argument and agreed with Wiart. Bellante must have thought that I, given the chance, would have sucker punched Wiart.

They wrested a few more commissions from us. They were very good, certainly as good as we were. I wondered if they would be better?

They repaired the spikes, and made replications of the face and foot for the museum. We were awarded the skin restoration. The Foundation held true to their word, and we were awarded Ellis Island, as part of a four company joint venture with Simpson as the leading business personality.

*New curl*

Aside from being the assistant director of the Metropolitan Museum's American Wing, Lewis Sharp was a noted scholar of the statuary of New York City, Central Park in particular. He surprised me when he called and said, "I have two favors to ask."

"Shoot."

"I want to see the Statue of Liberty up close. Can you take me there. Put me in Bruno's shoes? Can I bring an associate?"

"Sure, when do you want to go?"

"Sometime next week. Is that all right with you?"

"Anytime is good for me. What's the second thing?"

"We're having our annual dinner for the members of the William Cullen Bryant Fellows. We have different plan this year. John Chancellor, NBC News anchor will give the keynote address at the dinner on Friday night. Saturday we want to take the group for lunch on the yacht from the 23rd Street Pier. We hope that you'll give a lecture about your work on the Statue. We'll cruise by the Statue while you talk. Will you do it?

"I'm not a great public speaker, Lew."

"You'll be fine."

I took Sharp and his associate, James Pilgrim, to visit the statue on

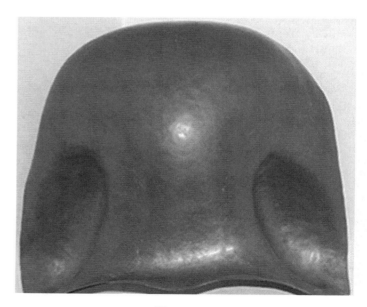

New nose

180

yet another lovely warm summer day. They enjoyed the scenes: boats played in the harbor; gulls flew by, Lady Liberty embraced them.

I asked Sharp if the philanthropic nature of the Bryant Fellows members could be petitioned by the Foundation? "How would you do that, Joe?"

"I did it with Dr. Ryskamp and Betty Wold Johnson. The Foundation provided their boat and box lunches, but we had a stormy day. It was pleasant enough given the storm."

The Foundation was grateful for this opportunity and had the head of fund raising, Denver Frederick call Sharp. Frederick had this down to a science. So did Sharp.

The black tie dinner at the Met was enjoyable. Sharp introduced Frederick to the audience. He made a short, simple request for donations to help save Miss Liberty. His request was later met with great munificence.

Mr. Chancellor was, as everyone knew, an exceptional speaker. He held his audience in pleasant rapture. I was supposed to follow this act?

The next morning, October 5, 1985 was rainy, windy and cold. Balinda, nine and half months pregnant and I arrived at the pier early. The captain stood in front of the gangplank and welcomed visitors. He looked at us and said, "Who are you?"

"I'm nobody," I said.

Sharp, behind me said, "He's my guest speaker."

The captain said, "The seas are too rough for her."

Sharp knew that Balinda had a lot of "Lucy" in her. I told them both how she had locked herself out of the house two weeks ago. She found a ladder and climbed into our second story bedroom. No big deal for her.

The captain didn't budge. Balinda was not going onto the high seas. The original plan had to be scrapped. Sharp worked out a new one. They would wait out the storm. Lunch and cocktails would be served and I would give the slide show lecture while in port. The ride around Manhattan would begin when the seas were normal.

The presentation went well. The banter of the question and answer period was personal and friendly. Before we left, a member of the group invited us back next year to introduce the baby to them. When Balinda was firmly on shore, the boat let out a collective sigh of relieve.

James Herbert Fiebiger was born the next day. Had he been a girl, she would have been named "Liberty."

# Chapter 23
## The Human Elements

The skin repair project encompassed: repairs to her skin; repair and reattachment of the lightning system; new interior gutters in the crown; new structural stainless steel to support the crown; new panels under the windows; implementation of system to expel puddled water; and patinization.

Most romantic were the skin repairs. Parts of her nose, eyes, lips, chin, shoulders, folds of fabric and chains had to be replaced. One curl needed total replacement. These parts were products of the times in which they were made. Their deepest cavities had been hammered to fragile thinness. There was no evidence

*A child from The Make A Wish Foundation visits the pendant of the torch*

of corrosion for causation of failure. Water entered the statue through Borglum's glazed torch. It ran down the sides and puddled in the lowest spots. Maintenance staff punched holes to allow the water to escape. The cause was mechanical, not atomic.

Once awarded the commission I asked Robbins and Bellante for permission to set up a patina farm. Robbins designated an area on the scaffolding near the area where the new torch would sit. Kaplan, photographed everything and was pleased to keep a photo journal as the migration of colors matured.

We hired Constance Bassett as our patinist. She was the first female subcontractor to work on the Statue. Bassett was a brown eyed, brown haired, pretty lady in her early thirties. She was gregarious, talented and efficient. She made fourteen samples, each from a different recipe. We mounted them as securely as possible and left them to time and Kaplan.

Bassett's recipes are at the end of this chapter.

LMC worked on the new torch. They beat their breasts as they beat their hammers. Proudly they affirmed that they were the only ones who followed traditional and timeless repoussé standards.

They never got the memo: the reason there were failures was that the hundred year old process was imperfect. It was as good as it could be for that point in time. The Foundation didn't want to replicate the past errors. No matter how innocent those errors were. Hopefully, there will be no need for restoration in 2086.

The empirical wisdom that we had garnered with the restoration of the copper roof for the Seman's family was valuable. We demonstrated to the Foundation in general and Robbins in particular that we could coax the copper, no matter how deep, without losing a thousandth of an inch.

Richard Knoor of Techno-Craft put together a team of talented foundry people, led by Bruce Hoheb and his daughter, Vanessa. Hoheb had a proprietary manner of taking negative impressions with plaster and with polymers that had memory. Meaning, if indexed properly, polymers could exactly replicate any form, regardless of undercuts.

This technology was the by-product of advances in dentistry. Anyone who ever discussed a new crown with his dentist had become familiar with the vocabulary and perhaps the process, albeit on a much smaller scale. An important aspect of the procedure was that shrinkage was limited to six ten thousands of an inch (.0006"). Meaning that the new parts would be 6/10,000 smaller than the original, the thickness of an average human hair. Obviously, too inconsequential to matter.

Once they had made the impressions, Knoor made synthetic males and females into and onto which copper could be hammered. He also made different hammer heads with the same polymers. The heads bounced back sometimes, but the thinness was prevented.

Ranieri and I had solved that problem long ago. We could hammer the copper into and onto the sides of the impressions. He monitored by sound. After some destructive testing, Ranieri was sure that he could monitor the thickness by the sounds the hammers made.

Another trick of the art, when using conventional stakes and hammers was to roll the wrist while the copper was struck.

The only rule we had was that we had no rules. There were no time restraints. The mandates were clear. Reproduce these parts better than they had been made. Not because we were better than the forefathers, simply because we lived in the space age. And we were curious!

The issue was the joinery, not the coaxing and humoring of the copper.

We made five noses. Some in five parts, some in three parts and one attempt at a monolithic piece. It merely proved that we too could thin the copper to tissue. We used 20th century devices and often resorted to the 19th century doming blocks and hammers.

Welding the joints was not the problem. Keeping the welded joints invisible was. We called welding experts, tried different combinations of gasses and wire rods. We welded, ground, filed, polished, applied chemical patinas, tested and tested. We put pieces in the freezer, buried them in the earth and put them on the roof.

We mixed oxygen, nitrogen and helium (85%, 14%, 1%) and brazed with deoxidized copper wire. We brazed with simple oxygen-acetylene, with various fluxes. All when tested left a minute tell tale hair line. It was most likely invisible to everyone but us.

Segundo Ruiz was an amazing welder. I often said, with humor, "He can weld plywood to aluminum." Had that been even remotely possible, Ruiz could have done it.

He welded a few pieces and had one of those industrial *eureka* moments. He thought the deoxidized copper rods worked okay, but that they didn't flow easily enough. He found a scrap piece of Romex wire laying on the floor. He peeled the plastic sheath and exposed the twelve gauge copper wire. He used it as a welding rod. The mixed gasses and the Romex wire produced an invisible weld. Not a trace of the weld could be found.

I mumbled to Ranieri, "Better to be lucky than good." He smiled, "Can you get that wire without the plastic on it?"

Ranieri made one nose from five parts. Ruiz welded them. We put the nose through our battery of rudimentary tests. All was well. I called Robbins and asked him to come to the shop and inspect it.

He arrived, as always sporting a smile and a bow tie. He brought a fascinating device with him. An electronic micrometer. We would have had to drill a hole in the nose for him to measure its thickness. This space age device was indeed magic.

He picked up a scrap of copper, passed the micrometer over, it read .0937", the approximate thickness when holding a dime and penny together. Then he passed it over a side of the nose, still .0930". He wandered lower, he read .0937." Finally he passed over the bottom of the nose, .0930". He smiled, "I really didn't think that you could do it. Pretty cool."

"How did you keep the welds invisible?"

"Do I have to tell you?" I asked.

He smiled as he read my mind. "Not now, but later you might want to write about it."

Robbins decided how he wanted to execute the replacement. There were a few options: replace the entire nose; replace the tip and nostrils as one assembly; replace the tip and both nostrils as three separate elements.

Replacement of the nose in its entirety would have been the most simple. The edges of the original joints were the same thickness as our nose, three thirty-seconds if an inch.

Robbins thought this inappropriate. Preservationists agreed with him. We would have removed too much original material just to make an easier joint. Robbins was pushing our talent envelope and I loved it.

We talked about how to make a mechanical connection. Despite our proven success with welded pieces he didn't want to pump immense amounts of heat into the skin. No reason to argue, we had another plan.

I explained how we did this type of joinery. I sited the stair railings for the

Senate Chamber in the Capitol. He understood *upsetting* the edges and planishing them together, using a common strip, called *astragal*.

It was a delicate surgical procedure. We had tolerances less than the thickness of a human hair. It was also forgiving, the materials could be gently coaxed.

A pilot project was in order. We mimicked those areas on the one piece nose that we had hammered to be too thin. We cut out approximate areas and cut replacement patches from one of other noses. Ranieri and Karhut hammered the edges upward, slightly deformed them while they were made thicker.

Another portion of a nose was used to cut out the *astragal* meeting surface. The inner surface of the nose was filed to allow smooth surfaces to mate. Ranieri had made copper rivets with small flat heads. They were bucked to hold the astragal to the new patch's *upset* surface.

Hardened steel hammer heads that we had rounded and polished were brought into play. Ranieri rubbed in circular motions while Karhut offered resistance. Slowly the deformed edges melded to one. They left it a little rough and completed the riveting procedures. Two pieces, one .0937" or an inch thick was bonded to a piece .0467", half the size. The bond was tight, invisible and reversible.

Bassett patinated it to an approximate color and we placed it in the freezer. After a week, we buried it in my tomato garden. Neither the joint nor the rivets could be seen.

Robbins and Bellante gave it their blessing and we made two more noses. One was given to the National Park Service with hope that they would never need it.

All the while both shops made armature bars, Smith passivated them and crews installed them. LMC made the beautiful new torch. They paid careful attention to our use of polymers and space age technology. I was surprised a few years later when they hired Hoheb as a sub-contractor.

While we made the easy parts for the eyes, lips, chin, ears, shoulders and chains we met CBS News anchorman Rolland Smith. Smith was filming a documentary of the restoration. Tall, handsome, charming and literate it was always a treat to share the day with him. He was insightful and diligent. I thought that he too, had grown to love the green lady in harbor. He coined a great phrase in his film, "...If pride had a sound, this was it...." We lunched one day and he asked, "Can I film Bruno and Micheli putting on the new nose?"

"Live?" I asked. "Yeah, live. Live on the mid day news."

My knees crumbled. I knew that Ranieri had ice water in his veins. He was afraid of nothing. But I sure was.

What if it didn't fit right? What if a wayward expletive slipped out?

I expressed all these feelings to him. He understood.

"How about if we just film it and use the clips later?"

Next the eyes and the left shoulder. Then the chains and adjacent lightening fixtures. Then Robbins threw us a curve.

One of Lady Liberty's curls had been found to require replacement. Patches wouldn't do, total replacement was mandated.

Cold weather approached quickly. Polymers that set up in the spring weather would not work in the cold. Robbins agreed that the curl could be removed from the statue and from Liberty Island if: it was transported with an armed guard for its four and two tenths of mile trip to our shop; was in the presence of an armed guard during off business hours; and it was returned immediately upon completion of the replication process.

Gonzalez an active member of the U.S. Army Reserve had a permit to carry a fire arm. Robbins trusted him to ride in the work bed of the truck with his gun and the curl. We could only travel mid day. Traffic would be light.

We disengaged the curl with great precision. We did the preponderance of the work one day and came back early the next to complete the task and comply with the mid day travel requirement.

We took the curl off, covered it with soft blankets and descended to grade on the construction elevator. The ever popular, Robert Kearney, elevator operator was laughing hard.

Kearney was special man. He operated the elevator and oversaw every-thing. He also helped children from The Make A Wish Foundation. He arranged, despite insurance entreaties to the contrary, for many children to fulfill their last wish: visit Lady Liberty, up close. Kearney sought out many different concierges. Executives, photographers, workers. I was honored to be chosen a few times.

Kearney took them all the way to top, to the shaft of the torch. They saw, what I believe is the best piece of art of the statue, the acanthus leaf pendant at the bottom of the torch. They also saw her face from an angle. Then he brought them to the base and allowed them to be gingerly escorted. Now they saw her right foot raised, heard the wind whistle lightly and saw her broken chains. The metaphor was explained to them. They had a personal experience with Lady Liberty like few others ever had. Most were caught in the ever present lens of Kaplan.

Most of the companies that were involved with the restoration had lapel pins made. It had become fashionable to collect them. Kearney had become a squirrel, he stashed them and he gave them to all the kids. Sad beyond belief, these were moments of unbridled love.

As we boarded the launch, the captain jokingly said, "no firearms allowed onboard."

When Gonzalez was secure in the rear of the truck, I said, "Keep the bullets in your pocket."

"I knew you would say that."

Under the watchful eye of an armed guard and German shepherd the curl slept very soundly that night.

The next day was consumed while Knoor and Hoheb's crew took impressions. This poor curl looked like she had lost a fight to Muhammad Ali. She was nonetheless, priceless. Once again, she slept soundly in the presence of her guard and dog. Next day, sans bullets, Gonzalez escorted her to the safety of Liberty Island.

The Hohebs made the non-shrinking impressions. Then they created the missing tip. Knoor then made negative and positive forms and we made a new curl. We made it in four pieces and held the thicknesses consistent.

Again Robbins took micrometer readings and again, there were no deviations. Ranieri, Karhut, Micheli and I went to install it on a very cold Saturday. The space was cramped and the joinery very time consuming. The three of them had it firmly in place and were bucking the rivets when we were told that the day's last launch would be leaving soon. Everyone was exhausted.

I didn't know why it was important that the curl be finished before Monday, but I trusted Robbins. If it weren't necessary, he wouldn't have been so insistent.

Ranieri said, "Do we really have to finish tomorrow? We're beat."

"No, they'll understand."

The temperature Sunday morning was around zero. The forecast was for the cold to continue and be mixed with snow. The only work that remained was the setting of approximately a hundred rivets. I dressed as warmly, went to the shop, picked up a small assortment of tools and went to see the green lady in my life.

The Hudson River was laden with ice floes, and the wind laced the water with white caps. I sat with the captain, warm in his pilot house. Ashore the wind doubled me over. I walked up the ramp and into the pedestal. I took the elevator to the to the base of the statue.

She and I were alone. I climbed the spiral stair from the base to her head and worked my way across the structural steel infrastructure to the curl. I was frightened as she swayed in the howling wind. I wondered if this was really only the three inches that was publicized.

My tasks were of kindergarten proportion. A hammer in each hand and rivet in between. The concussion expanded the shafts of the rivets inside the holes and the connections were secure.

Frozen, I lumbered back to down to launch. The captain opened the door and said, "You were quick. Want some coffee?"

Before I answered he handed me a cup. A mate threw the rope on deck and he gently glided through the ice floes.

"Do you know what they call you? He asked.

"I don't want to know."

"Some guys love you, others don't. They say you're the conscience of the statue."

"Is that good or bad?"

"I don't know." He said. "Big job like this, lots of personalities, big egos."

We docked, I thanked him and left.

I was glad that he had been on our Christmas gift list. A bottle of scotch could keep a fellow warm in this weather.

The system to arrest lightning was a network of five-eighths of inch round copper bars that led to the river bed. They had been soldered in place. Lightning strikes had melted the solder away and the bars were unattached in many areas.

The areas that had been struck by lightening were scarred. Areas of skin had bubbles under the patina and the patina itself was multi-colored. The areas looked bruised. Their interior counterparts had a residue of the solder that had melted. We called this "Fried Lightning."

Reattachment via soldering made sense. The heat needed to solder would inflict minor damage to the patina, but the trade was worthwhile.

We had numerous scars that were to be touched up by Bassett when the patinization phase began. These just added to the list.

Eutectic Corporation had an exceptional alloy solder. It contained cadmium which meant that respirators had to be worn when using it. It flowed at four hundred degrees and was exceptionally strong. An added benefit was that the flux was buried in the core of the solder. The round copper bars were heated with oxygen-acetylene torches, the heat transferred to the skin and the solder flowed to make strong connections. The amount of heat was so insignificant that the patina was barely affected. DelVecchio and Assas perfected this system of reattachment. Their tasks were made easier with the use of walkie-talkies.

The theoretical thickness of the skin was three-thirty seconds of an inch. That is only one thirty-second of an inch less than one eighth. Underwriters Laboratories had done extensive tests to determine the thickness of lightning rods, called "air terminals." They determined that a nominal thickness of one eighth of an inch would arrest lightning. Therefore, the Statue of Liberty was her own lightning rod.

The weep holes that had been punched in the areas where water puddled, required repair. We designed a grommet with a flange. The washer like flange had grooves machined in them to prevent puddling. We machined grommets of various sizes to accommodate the variety of ragged holes.

DelVecchio and Assas found the right diameter shaft, inserted them and riveted the flanges to the skin. The tips of the round straw like pieces were then gently hammered, like rivets to hide the rough edges.

<hr>

William Geist, a reporter for the *New York Times*, interviewed me in June 1984. We chatted conversationally. I explained the history of the blacksmith. What an amazing and creative fellow he has always been. He made all the tools for both farms and workshops. Necessity was the mother of invention to him. He harnessed water to drive his hammer. He was healer of sorts with smoke from his fires. Maybe I bored him.

But I got his interest when I said. "The great Michelangelo was first a smith and then a sculptor."

"Why?" Geist queried.

"He didn't want to trust too much to others. He learned to forged and temper his chisels."

He chose to edit my words to the point of my embarrassment.

I learned a valuable lesson. Whether or not I could implement that knowledge, I didn't know.

The restoration almost complete, I spoke with another reporter. He asked, "Was this the commission of a lifetime?"

My guard went up and I recoiled. I thought and he repeated his question.

"It was the job of three lifetimes, my grandfather and father held my hand all the way."

The Foundation was gracious. They gave Certificates that thanked each person for his or her contribution to the restoration. Everyone cherished it.

LMC lofted their beautiful, gold leafed torch in place and the Restoration of the Statue of Liberty was completed.

I, like many, many others had fallen in love with her. I figured she loved me too. I had fallen from the scaffolding and somehow she intercepted my fall. It was cold that day and I went to kiss her on the lips to say "thanks." I got stuck to her and needed two tubes of Chap Stik.

Another time I had been careless and seen stars when my head hit one of her spikes. She and the hard hat saved me. That made three, I remembered how she saved my right hand.

She saved a lot of us. Men had suffered minor burns, bruises and cuts, but thankfully, nothing major.

I had ridden in the back of launch returning to Manhattan while the sun was setting on Liberty's head. Gorgeous in any light, she was specially appealing. I was talking with Robbins and Landsman, each of us enjoying the moment.

I said to no one in particular, "Its too bad you can only climb up the inside."

Robbins glanced a curious eye toward me.

"Too bad we can't let people see her the we way did. Have a love affair with her. We were lucky."

Robbins shook his head, "We were lucky. But you better shut up, they'll burn you a the stake."

I shut up. Heresy or not, I couldn't stop thinking about it. Not many people know the chains are there. No one ever sees them.

Visitors climb 354 stairs to the crown. The area is well lit and the journey is pleasant for some. Claustrophobic for others. The ventilation system always pumps clean air. One can marvel at Eiffel's genius when studying the armature network. Some enjoy the inside views of the copper.

When they reach the crown, 260 feet above the river, Voilà, New York's skyline and harbor greet them. It has been said by many, "This is a moment that I will remember forever." Some do. The march of travel continues at the pace of the crowd, this time downward.

Imagine, I mused, if visitors had an external viewing arena. This would be set 155 feet above the river, where the statue meets the top of the pedestal. Wide spiral stairs, cleverly heated in winter, would allow unrestricted climbing speeds. Access for handicapped people would be provided by an elevator.

The promenade would need to be a major collaborative effort of architects and engineers. I imagine a structural steel and glass promenade with two spiral staircases and elevator set at the rear. The promenade would not be seen from afar.

The project would be handled in accordance with standards for conservation and preservation. Materials removed, i.e., field stone, structural steel, etc., would archived. The project would be reversible. Unwanted in the future, it could be removed.

Visitors would enter the promenade on the Lady's right side, and would be greeted by her raised foot. Would they feel her stepping forward?

Armed with 21st century audio and visual devices, they would listen to an informative voice while they looked upward with binoculars. Photo op areas would be established and groups could have their photos with a variety of backgrounds.

Perhaps photos taken of families with both the chains and Manhattan in the background would be a favorite.

Imagine the setting. You have walked past her sandal, looked up at her, felt her presence. You stood on this warm, sun filled day in front of her chains. Gentle breezes tumbled your hair and your clothing, they whistled softly around her legs. Gulls flew by. The two of you share the views Manhattan's skyline and the harbor at work and play.

You have been treated to feel her power, grace, dignity and beauty as never before.

You have just fallen in love.

We know how Gaget and Gauthier worked the copper in the 19th century and we know how LMC and our firm worked it in the 20th century. You may be interested to think ahead to such copper work in the 21st century.

You must accept that the forefather's of the art were always pushing technology's envelope.

Unchanged, the sculptor would create his one quarter size machete in what ever medium he or she liked best, clay, wax, plaster, Styrofoam, etc.

Computer power would digitally enlarge the model and shake hands with a five axis milling machine.

Large polyurethane blocks would be placed on the bed of the milling machine. The cutting stylus would carve a negative cavity.

Hydro forming is a process where high pressure water forces the copper into a form. No heat, no magic wax, no hammering, no scratches, no loss of original luster, perhaps no work hardening.

The proper size copper sheet would be clamped over the die and the doors of the machine would be closed. Water nozzles would deliver as much as ten thousand pounds per square inch of pressure while coaxing the copper to seat in the form. The time required to form a piece, three minutes.

Many various fabrication methods would be available. The lower levels of a thick gauge with the thicknesses lightened as it worked upward. Copper pieces could be made with return flanges, each precisely mated to its neighbor. The flanges could be riveted, bolted or welded. This assumes that the hydro forming process yield a sharp corner at the bend. Any radius to that bend would be unforgivable as it would create a shadow line.

Alternative methods would allow for lap joints, similar to the original. Another approach would be to have a very small flange created that faced outward. When mated, the slight protrusions would be used as a welding rod, the joints neatly "zipped" by the welder.

One wonders if an armature network would even be necessary.

How much fun it would be.

# *Lady Liberty's Technical Needs*

## PREPARATION OF THE METAL
### STATEMENT OF INTENT

P.A. Fiebiger. Inc. was asked to prepare prototype pieces for replacement armature elements in the Statue of Liberty. The treatments and recommendation outlined below are meant only as suggestions based on our present understanding of the problem.

Four pieces of mild steel were hand forged to specific configurations. based on patterns provided by the Committee. Stresses that developed in working the steel were relieved by annealing. Select pieces were drilled. tapped, chamfered, and micro-blasted by sand (1/4 grade) and aluminum oxide. These steps were intended to duplicate the kinds of operations that would be carried out on actual armature and support elements used in the Statue of Liberty.

### ELECTRO-PLATING: THE PRINCIPLE

The electro-plating of iron is a standard technique for protection against corrosion under exposure to a hostile environment. Iron electroplated with successive layers of copper and a tin-nickel alloy represent a state of the art treatment. It has been well documented in extensive tests carried out by the Tin Institute and others, and is accepted as a standard technique for corrosion prevention in many industrial applications.

The principle of the treatment is based on the noncorrosive nature of the tin-nickel alloy. Iron itself is readily susceptible to oxidation. and converts to an iron oxide (rust). A tin-nickel alloy will remain stable in corrosive environments such as the conditions anticipated in the Statue of Liberty. If the iron is plated with a tinnickel alloy, the outer skin will protect the iron. However, in the event of any micro-porosity or mechanical damage to the tin-nickel, the iron would rapidly corrode at those points, especially in the presence of the more noble tinnickel alloy. The purpose of the copper inter-layer is to prevent the chance of such corrosion. A thick. ductile layer of copper effectively plugs up any micro-porosity. preventing migration of water to the iron substrate. It also provides protection against me-chanical abrasion of the tinnickel. In terms of electrolytic corrosive activity, both the tin-nickel and iron will be sacrificed in preference to the more noble copper metal. Since the tin-nickel alloy is stable. it prevents the copper from changing its electrical state and protects the copper. The iron is totally covered with copper and is effectively sealed from oxygen and cannot convert to rust. This, in brief. explains the long term stability of the iron, copper, tin-nickel system. It protects the steel from corroding. without altering the mechanical properties of the steel in terms of its elasticity. flex~ etc.

**ELECTRO-PLATING: THE TREATMENT**

The four pieces were first plated with a thick layer of copper. This assures com-plete coverage of the steel surface. Also, it provides some ductility to the protective skin as the steel goes through the dimensional changes and deformations antici-pated at the Statue of Liberty. The second layer is a tin-nickel alloy, which acts as the noncorrosive skin. as explained above.

A final layer of copper is plated on top of the tin-nickel alloy. The purpose of this skin is to protect the copper plates in the event of contact with an armature element. An exposed tin-nickel surface might accelerate corrosion of a copper surface with which it is in contact. By plating with a final layer of copper, all points of contact between the copper plates and the armature elements are in the most compatible and least corrosive states, since no dissimilar metals are present. Only copper is in contact with copper.

If another metal (ie: Ferralium) is used in place of iron, there may be concern for the long term characteristics of this metal while in contact with copper. Further consideration must be given to its relationship with other metal elements, i.e. mechanical fasteners. The necessary equilibrium can be assured via electo-plating the Ferralium with copper.

## RECOMMENDATION ON THE USE OF INDIUM

It is recommended that an inter-layer of Indium, either in sheet or plated on the surface, be used between all bolts and overlapping sections of metal. Indium has a large inherent plastic flow under compression. even at the temperature conditions anticipated at the Statue of Liberty. As such, it will tend to fill all voids and afford complete coverage between the two surfaces in which it is applied. Even as the metal sections move. and the bolts expand and contract in place, the Indium will continue to 'flow' under compression. filling all voids. It assures intimate contact between surfaces at all times. Indium is an excellent oxygen scavenger. In this capacity, it will preferentially take up any oxygen in preference to the other metals present, thus preventing corrosion of the copper in which it is in contact.

Because of the cold flow and oxygen scavenging properties of Indium. it will afford protection at those points most susceptible to corrosion. Without Induim. exposed copper surfaces will convert to copper sulfate and iron to rust. The constant expansion and contraction of the metal support pieces and bolts will create voids which, if not filled. will permit corrosion at these points. Indium acts to fill these voids. As a double protection. it will scavenge any oxygen that is present in preference to the other metals present.

January 13. 1984 Submitted by:

Steven Weintraub, Associate Conservator. Objects Conservation, The Metropolitan Museum of Art, New York. NY.

Richard Smith, President, Group Research, Inc., 247 Center Street, New York, NY

# Procedure For Patinization of Replacement
## and
# Repaired Elements on the Statue of Liberty

By Constance K Bassett

Application procedure for developing various antique green patinas:

The copper sheeting surface with a dilute or form is solution of:

nitric acid – 1 part

distilled water  - 25 parts

or by lightly bead or sand blasting.

The copper is washed with a dilute solution of

ammonium sulfide 1

distilled water 10 parts

darkening the metal to an even shade of brown-black.  The metal is rinsed with distilled water,  neutralizing the chemical. The copper is allowed to dry. The surface is now prepared for the green patination.

I.   Plaques 1 - 4

These plaques were washed successively with a solution of:

ammonium chloride –1 part

distilled water  -17 parts

The surface was allowed to dry between coats

II.  Plaques 5 - 8

These plaques were washed successively with a solution of

cupric nitrate -1 part

ammonium chloride -1 part

calcium chloride -1 part

distilled water  -17 parts

The surface was allowed to dry between coats. When a light green was achieved, the patina was finished with -successive coats of Solution I (plaques 5-7). Plaque 8 was washed repeatedly with Solution II, only.

III. Plaques 9 - 10

These plaques were washed successively with a solution of:

cupric nitrate -2 parts

ammonium sulfide -1 part

calcium chloride -5 parts

distilled water -17 parts

The surface was allowed to dry between coats. When a blue-green was achieved, the patina was finished with several coats of Solution I.

IV. Plaques 11-14

These plaques were washed successively with a of:

cupric chloride -1 part

ammonium chloride -1 part

distilled water - 34 parts

The surface was allowed to dry between coats.

Constance Bassett

Moorland Studios, Inc.

25 S. Main Street

Stockton, New Jersey 08559

## *Chapter 24*
## *Ellis Island*

Faithful to their pledge, in late November 1984, the Foundation asked us to assist with the study and storage of all of the decorative copper ornaments from the roof and domes of the Main Building of Ellis Island.

The seven-acre farm that Samuel Ellis sold in 1808 was enlarged seventy-five years later to twenty-two acres. Three million six hundred thousand cubic yards of earth were removed when New York carved its first subway. Much of that was used to enlarge the island.

Architects Edward Tilton and William Boring designed the French Renaissance buildings and grounds. The main building was noted for its red brick and limestone facade and decorative copper domes. The story of Ellis Island is not found in the buildings, it is found in stories of the twelve million immigrants that passed through.

If only the walls could talk. The Restoration of Ellis Island

*Ellis Island*

resuscitated the pathos and ethos that had lay silent in the bricks and plaster for eighty-years.

Lehrer/McGovern had been awarded the contract to be the construction manager. Construction management was replacing general construction. The construction manager as agent for the owner, had a modest profit, between one and two percent, guaranteed. All expenses, pencils, paper, paper clips, telephone calls and salaries to name but a few, were paid. The issue for debate was whether or not the general contractor, now the manager could perform better with his risk obviated.

McGovern's superintendent was Sandy Ginsberg. He was a talented, all business guy  who managed to squeeze eighty minutes into the hour. When he came up long enough to take a breath he proved himself to open minded and fair.

The Foundation had designated Larry Bellante and Ziva Benderly to serve Ellis and the Statue of simultaneously. They did both, it seemed to me, with great dedication, ease and efficiency.

The Historical Architect for the National Park Service was an early thirties man, Peter Dessauer.  Ever the fastidious Southern gentlemen, he was of average height, athletic build and brilliant mind.

Dessauer, Callirgos and Knoor along with a group from our shop went to the Main Building on a freezing day in mid January 1985. The building had been abandoned in 1954.

Residents here were nocturnal creatures, sea gulls and the spirits of those who had passed here before. The gulls came and went through the door-less portals. Evidence of rodents was obvious. Overpowering were the spirits.

Long before we looked at the copper pieces we felt the spirits' presence. An escort told us that we were passing the area where the notorious eye loop procedure was performed. If a potential immigrant had pink eye, he or she was denied admission. I shuddered as I felt the fear of so many.

*Display of the original ornamentation*

We walked through the laundry and saw huge pieces of equipment. The mangle was so frightening that I thought that the name was a *double entendre*.

We walked down a hall from the laundry to kitchen and saw a machine that was slender and very long. Our escort, seeing the inquisitive looks on our faces offered, "It might be the first computer in America."

"How'd it work?" Asked Ranieri.

"Every person had a card, the card had holes punched in designated spots to provide information. The cards were passed through a system of rods and were sorted. All mechanical. Pretty cool, huh?"

Not only was it cool, it was freezing. The spirits followed us wherever we went.

Dessauer offered some history as we walked. "The island was closed in 1954. In 1978 the Park Service took all of these parts off and tried to seal the domes with stucco."

"We're here," he said, as we entered the staging area.

Dessauer had supervised the collection of hundreds of pieces of the copper that made the whole. It was an immense body of work.

The majority of them were *rope stampings*. Some of elements were spun and others were brake sections. All were tissue paper thin. I took micrometer readings, twenty-one thousandths (.021") of an inch thick, twenty-four gauge. The approximate thickness of three to five pieces of human hair.

Each piece had been ravaged by time and the elements.

Everyone involved in the work was fully literate in the history of *rope stampings*. They had all visited our shop and watched us make the pieces for the Semans' roof. They visited the roof and they liked our method.

We made faithful reproductions that were over twice the thickness of the originals. The original pieces required armatures of either wood or iron for support. Ours, as independent chassis needed no armature network. Their strength was imposed by the curves and the thickness.

Our welding techniques had developed exponentially. These pieces would be welded and the joints would not discolor.

The Statue of Liberty was all repoussé work, handwork. Ellis was all machine work. Each was restored as it had been made, save for technological advances that assured fragile features would not be repeated.

As had the Statue, Ellis suffered major damage in the 1913 Black Toms sabotage explosion. Dessauer's drawings differentiated between pre and post explosion pieces. Post explosion replications had slight variations. We made versions of both.

A temporary construction bridge was erected from Liberty State Park to the island. Frozen and tired we left the island in cars and trucks. Knoor, Assas, Del Vecchio and Gonzalez met a group from Dessauer's office the next few days to chose and transport the pieces. Knoor evaluated them all and chose the best pieces from which to reproduce the replicas.

All this work and we didn't have a contract yet. McGovern wanted to keep us attached to Simpson. Simpson's union power was important. Simpson chose to use his Simpson Metal Industries rather than NAB. He

*View of the dome and globe, facing the Statue of Liberty*

also wanted to spread the risk and brought in two friendly competitors, Fred A. Munder and Leonard Kent. The four of us would make the quadraventure, Simpson, Munder, Fiebiger and Kent (SMFK).

Munder and Kent were charming, knowledgeable men and I pleased to be associated with them. Simpson had decided to make his thirty-year-old son, Gary, project manager.

A handsome young man with bright blue eyes and an inviting smile, that he chose to use sparingly. He was a chip off the old block,.

The copper roofs of the buildings could have been measured in acres. I understood the need for a different mentality. I still wanted the famous Dodgers manger of the '50s, Leo Dorocher to be wrong with his famous quip, "Nice guys finish last."

The apparent custom of big contractors was to have the bid preparations run late into the night. These were catered affairs. Simpson, Munder, Kent, Einbinder and I met for a few of these events. We talked, absent of Simpson. When we had apportioned a number to a category, Simpson was called from his office to give his blessing. The odds always varied on his ruling, but you could have bet your house that his ruling was to be different than our opinions. Munder and Kent got upset when he sliced too much off of a budget category. This was déjà vu. I was just glad that the food was good.

We hit a major snag with the domes. The architectural drawings for the domes made no provision for the effects of Oscillation 101. There were no expansion joints.

Once more, I climbed on my soapbox and explained the teachings of the Office of the Architect of the Capitol. They all listened carefully and found it plausible. Simpson remembered that George M. White, Architect of the Capitol was a consultant to the Foundation.

I lobbied to call this omission to their attention now. I argued that we should design the expansion joints now and present the remedy and the costs.

I argued that we were assured of this job; it wasn't competitive and we should show our good faith.

"Good faith," bellowed Simpson. "Do you still believe in the Easter Bunny, Joe"

"Not the Bunny, but Santa," I said.

"Joe, other roofers are bidding this. Believe me, I know. We are in competition. Forget the expansion joints. We'll get an extra for them."

"Ed, it's a big ticket item. We owe them at least to call it to their attention."

Angry with me, he said, "Damn it Joe, just drop it!"

Einbinder and I talked about it later. "Ed doesn't think that you'll ever learn."

"He's right. What's to learn? I'm not being stubborn, I'm just being me." He smiled that professorial smile.

Callirgos again showed his genius. He designed a very intricate skeletal network of stainless steel angles to hold the copper pieces.

Knoor continued to feed us mated dies to deep draw pieces of copper. The process had a nice rhythm. The work piece coated with its magic Johnsons 7000 wax, the hum of the press, and the coaxing of the copper. Interrupted to be annealed, the noise and heat of the large torches, followed the by steam and hissing of it being quenched. Seven to ten passes were required to form one piece.

We had assigned a few men to this work while most of the others worked either of the armature bars or body parts of the Statue. A large inventory was growing.

Round pieces that had been *spun* originally were sub-contracted to metal spinning companies for reproduction. Metal spinning is a very old and proven method to make hollow, round objects. Parts for lighting fixtures, household goods, urns, bells, cylinders-the list is endless. A form is mounted in a lathe. A metal disk is fastened to the form and rotated at high speeds. A mechanic applies force to the disk with levers. He changes the fulcrum to gain various mechanical advantages.

The spires atop the domes were critical. They had to extremely strong and also be lightning rods. They qualified because they met the Underwriter Laboratories one eighth of an inch thickness requirement. Seventeen feet, eight inches tall, they tapered from twelve inches at the top to twenty four inches at the base. They sat 133 feet above grade.

Once again, we enlisted the expertise of Gerson Feiner. A big man, with a big smile and bigger heart he was always ready to help. His grandfather and Opa were friends and had worked together. We both lived in Westchester County,

I called him and explained the situation. "Come for dinner, I'll ask Shirley to put more water in the soup. Bring drawings."

No soup that night. He studied the drawings and was up to speed in a heartbeat. "Joe, nobody can make these in one piece, it's gotta be made in two halves. We'll have to  it on the brake."

"Are you sure you can do this?"

"Have I ever let you down?" He asked.

I smiled and shook my head.

He and his staff had to develop a pattern for the work piece. Accurate calculation the angles to coax this partial ice cream cone into shape paramount. The margin for error was slight. Feiner had a hydraulic

*Gennaro "Bruno" Ranieri stands proudly with the completed spires*

brake with a bed of sufficient size to allow the work piece to be placed *out of square* to the blade. They had the talent to do it.

They made the pieces to perfection. Like the columns at the Capitol, they were made in longitudinal halves with the seams flawlessly welded.

Hundreds of stamped parts were trimmed, assembled, welded, ground and polished. These sub-assemblies decorated the spire.

Fifteen men worked to stamp, trim, assemble, weld, grind and polish the hundreds of decorative elements. Necessity had made us grow larger than I liked. Something just didn't feel right. I stopped to take our collective temperature. Safety first.

I called a firm of *industrial hygienists* to evaluate our work environment. The first question their representative asked was, "How many different languages are spoken?" I had to think a moment, "English, Italian, German and Spanish," I said.

Their counselor announced himself in the office and asked if he could make a tour of the shop. I introduced him to each man. He spoke to them in their native languages and took copious notes.

Back in the office he explained the routine. "Industrial hygiene is an immerging field, far too long in coming. I'm going to put little monitoring devices on each man, the devices relate to tasks that he performs. I'll come back and get them next week. About two weeks after that, I'll have the results."

"What's your early blush?" I asked.

"I'm glad to see that you don't blast with sand and that you have a fresh air supply for the blasting. You have the proper respirators and safety equipment and good first aid system."

He asked, "What is a problem that you would like resolved?"

"I don't know if this is in your bailiwick. We use nylon lifting slings rather than wire rope slings. The slings have *telltale* warnings built into them to call attention to their need for replacement. When they get worn, they are soft and easy to use. But nobody throws them out. I have to burn them to get rid of them. Any suggestions?"

"Your right, that's a behavioral thing. Just should keep burning them."

Two weeks later, he came back with a big smile. I asked, "Well, how are we?"

"Everybody's okay, two minor problems," he said.

My heart pounded, "Oh my God, I have hurt someone?" I exclaimed.

"Nothing severe, two of the fellows have 'copper disease.'"

"Copper disease. What is it?"

"They may itch once in a while, that's all."

"Do you itch?" He asked me. "I should have tested you too. You're exposed to everything."

Years later I wished that I had let him.

The *industrial hygiene* experience was worth much more than the twenty-five hundred dollar fee. It should be mandatory in the workplace. Another of my father's bromides was true, "There's no good business in bad business."

Iron Worker's Local 580 had installed the elaborate stainless steel network that supported the copper. Sheet Metal Worker's Local 28 had installed all of the copper. Our staff, when on the island were only permitted to inspect and advise.

A full size prototype of the dome had been constructed. Save for the spire, The decorative pieces that went around the base of the dome were the Bead and Real that was attached to base of Cartouché. The attachment was made per the original scheme.

I monitored this closely. Despite winter conditions, the oscillating dome had moved. Simpson arranged with the unions to allow us to conduct very rudimentary tests to support our hypothesis. We managed to demonstrate that at ground level, in February, the dome moved seven-thirty seconds of an inch, almost a quarter of inch.

George M. White, as an advisor to the Foundation was asked to comment. He and other architects and engineers inspected the prototype and agreed. The dome was a body in motion.

Dessauer asked them to visit our shop to determine an appropriate remedy. George White, John Belle, Henry Herb, Ziva Benderly, Larry Bellante, Milton Einbinder, Victor Callirgos and Peter Dessauer met in our shop. Everyone was given coffee while Ranieri and Karhut assembled the large Bead and Reel assemblies to the bases of the Cartouchés.

Someone said, "I thought that since they were at the base that they would be exempt from the motion?'

"Good try." I thought.

The group was off to the side, huddling next to a radiator for additional warmth. I gave my now familiar soapbox performance of Oscillation 101, attributing, of course this knowledge to Mr. White's office.

White was so cool! He had the floor and everyone waited. He smiled and said, "He's right." His body language said, "You should have known that."

I imagined him to say, "How's a baboon like Joe know this and you don't."

Callirgos passed around sketches of his proposed solutions. Ranieri had made a few prototypes, he and Karhut set them in place.

Dessauer knew of my early warning to my venture partners. He agreed with me, we should have presented it when we knew it. All this did was delay things and make it cost more. The remedy would allow the dome to inexorably follow the setting sun without allowing water to enter.

We made matched sets of twenty-four inch square plates, one inch thick to attach the spire to the building. One plate was made with iron and copper plated, the other of copper. Richie Smith plated the iron pieces with copper to assure an interface between the similar metals.

Ranieri and I had worried about Local 580's ability to set the plates with pristine accuracy. The plates were fastened to the structural steel of the dome. One or two degrees off would represent a problem.

Always those belts and suspenders. We had two choices. We could wait to drill the holes in the copper plate or we could drill the holes and make the adjustment when we welded the spire to plate. We chose the later.

Einbinder, Callirgos, and Ranieri made templates to assure the orientation of the ornaments to points of the compass.

There are two ways to weld objects to plates, an easy way and hard way. When I explained our procedure to Simpson he said, "Why did I know that you'll do it the hard way?"

"Its really the only way."

I guess he knew that I would not be deterred. We took the long route. We asked Feiner to machine eighteen inch diameter tapered holes in the copper plate. We wanted a tight, friction fit as the shaft of the spire passed through the base plate.

Ranieri, Karhut and Ruiz set the plates to the alignment templates with great care. Ruiz welded both the inside and outside surfaces. The connection was strong.

The spires and the globes that followed were to be installed with a helicopter. We designed a lifting cradle that served two purposes: it assured safe over the road transportation; and it pivoted upward to allow the helicopter to fetch it easily.

Though we often made too much noise, we tried to be good neighbors. We made charitable contributions, sponsored Golden Gloves, repaired broken parts of stoves and bicycles. The small town aspect of New York City showed its loving face. Two large flat bed trucks announced to the neighborhood that something was about to happen. A crowd of silent observers had gathered at the exit of our yard on thirty sixth street. As the loaded flatbeds pulled out every one applauded. Time stood still, I looked to

Ranieri, he, like I, had tears in his eyes.

The insurance carrier for the Foundation insisted that the spires be fitted with flotation devices. The Coast Guard provided the appropriate hardware and the first spire was lifted from its cradle. It was like watching a surgical procedure in a very large operating theatre.

The helicopter hovered above, let its cable and hook down to an assistant. He took it, fastened it securely to a device that we had made and backed away. As the pilot continued to hover, he engaged the winch and slowly, very slowly the spire began to rotate from horizontal.

Vertical, it was freed from the cradle and lifted upward. Crews atop the first dome waited. As if by magic, the pilot hovered directly over the center of the dome. The spire was lowered and men disconnected the flotation devices. The winch was lowered inch by inch as it found its way home. The entire procedure took thirteen minutes.

We repeated it three more times.

How proud everyone was as this delicate piece of copper jewelry found its place in the skyline.

Next up, the eight foot diameter spun ornamental globes. They too would serve as lightning rods, therefore they were made of one eighth inch thick material.

The Kosempel Manufacturing Company in Philadelphia was the only company able to make such large pieces. A company representative told me the he thought that this was one of largest spinnings ever made in the United States.

Callirgos had prepared detailed drawings for the completed globe. They required no armature due to their one eighth of inch thickness, but they required a lifting cradle built into them.

The joints along the equators were to be welded. Decorative fenders with pointed caps concealed the joints.

Callirgos and I drove to Philadelphia to watch them make the first

*Signature plaque with names of all the artisans that made the decorative copper elements*

hemisphere. As we drove I explained the mechanics of the process that I had witnessed on a smaller scale. The work piece was spun at the desired revolutions per minute, an operator placed different levers against posts whose spacing changed the amount of force required.

I kidded Callirgos, "Watch, we're gonna see twenty-five guys pulling on a long wooden arm. They'll probably be outside of the building." The enormity of this undertaking was not being taken for granted.

Callirgos said, "I hope you're not too serious."

We turned into the plant and I said with a laugh, "Do you see all those guys?"

We didn't know what to expect when we entered. A company representative welcomed us, "I guess you want to see how we're dong this? Everybody else does." He led to an appendix of the shop.

The room was well lit and housed one machine. One man operated it. The disk was being rotated at eight RPMs. There was no tachometer to determine it, the operator made a soapstone (chalk) line and looked at his watch. A hydraulic cylinder replaced the large lever that my fictitious twenty-five men used. The operator set it in contact with the disk and forced it to the form.

Callirgos and I had a fun class trip. Somewhere on the Jersey Turnpike on the way home, he said, "I'm always amazed how creative some guys are."

"Me too."

The fenders were essentially copper troughs, six feet long, twelve inches wide and two inches deep. They were difficult to make due their compound shapes and lengths. They would not fit in our press and would have had to be made in three pieces and welded. There had to a more efficient way.

I sought the advice of a local automotive body shop. I took one of the original pieces to Manhattan Collision's general manager and showed it to him.

"How many do you need?" He questioned.

"Forty."

"Easy enough," he said.

"How," I replied.

"*English wheel*. All the coach works have'em. Takes some training, but a good operator can stretch and shrink fenders and doors. I have friend who makes stretch limos. He's out on Long Island, he'll do'em easy as pie. You'll just have give him the materials. I don't think he ever worked with copper before, but, hey, metal's metal."

A construction helicopter lifted the globes into place and Ellis Island was completed.

On one of spires, under the urn and invisible to any observer, is an engraved plaque with the date and names of all the artisans who had done this work.

# *Epilog*

Arthritis began to show its ugly head in early '90s. I watched in disbelief as my joints betrayed me. Orthopedists who knew of my active business career told me that I was a danger to myself and to those around me.

We had finished the first phase of Ryskamp's restoration plan at The Frick. He was pleased with it and wanted to talk with me. As I limped into his office, he said, "I'm worried about you, Joe. You always look pained."

"I try not to show it, I guess I'm not good at that yet."

"Sit down."

He grimaced as he watched me ease into a chair and said, "What can I do to help you? You've been to the best doctors, I presume?"

"I have. It's not a pretty picture any way you look at it. They say that I'm riddled with lead, copper and cadmium. The heavy metals may have caused the arthritis to come early. They can change hips and shoulders, but not necks and backs. They all advise a high, dry climate."

"Are you fifty yet? " he asked.

" Forty-seven." I answered.

"I've met your family and I certainly have grown to know you through the years. My suggestion to you, though you haven't asked is, 'family first'. You've had a great career. The City owes your firm a debt of gratitude, I certainly do."

Untypical of me, I interrupted him, "No, Dr. Ryskamp, I am in your debt." He got up and came from behind his desk and put his hand on my shoulder, I rose.

He said, "Nothing is forever, take care of your family. Let me know if I can ever help."

I thanked him for everything and left with teared eyes. He followed me to the door and said, "I still want you to write your book. Brooke (Astor) and Bunny (Mellon) will love it. I'll edit for you. I'm serious, Joe. The stories are part of the art."

"You'll be fine. Remember, if you need me, call."

I had turned toward him, smiled weakly and said, "I really appreciate that."

Charles Ryskamp, eighty-one died in April 2010, two months before I competed this book.

# *Credits For Photographs*

*Front Cover*
*Fotolia: ©Gary #5278299*

*Page 1*
*The young man on the right is Paul James Fiebiger*
*Photo: P.A. Fiebiger, Inc.*

*Page 2*
*Southeast Corner of Tenth Avenue and 36th Street*
*Before construction of the Lincoln Tunnel*
*Ca. 1932*
*Photo: P.A. Fiebiger, Inc.*

*Page 3*
*462 Tenth Avenue Shop*
*Man in the center is a more mature Paul James Fiebiger*
*Ca. 1923*
*Photo: P.A. Fiebiger, Inc.*

*Page 10*
*Hand forged angel of peace*
*Ca. 1290*
*Photo: P.A. Fiebiger, Inc.*

*Page 13*
*Hand forged chandeliers*
*Photo: P.A. Fiebiger, Inc.*

*Page 14*
*Hand carved wood pulpit with hand forged iron lectern*
*Photo: P.A. Fiebiger, Inc.*

*Page 17*
*Photo: Wikimedia Commons*
*Photographer: Ad Meskens*

*Page 21*
*Presidential Seal*
*Pre Truman Administration*
*Drawing: P.A. Fiebiger, Inc.*

*Page 21*
*Presidential Seal*
*Post Truman Administration*
*As a work of the U.S. federal government, the image is in the public do-*
*main.*
*Extracted from the title page of PDF document at http://www.whitehouse.*
*gov/nsc/nss.pdf*
*Author: Unknown*

*Page 23*
*Hand forged & repoussé gate & fanlight*
*Photo: P.A. Fiebiger, Inc.*

*Page 25*
*Directoiré Stair Railing*
*Page Cross, Architect*
*Photo: P.A. Fiebiger, Inc.*

*Page 29*
*21 Club*
*Creative Commons Attribution 2.5 Generic license*
*Photographer: David Shankbone*

*Page 33*
*Louis XVI hand forged & repoussé stair railing*
*New York City Residence*
*Designed by Jean Balbous & Joseph Fiebiger*
*Photo: Courtesy of Mrs. Enid A. Haupt*

*Page 36*
*Modern stair railing*
*Palm Beach Residence*
*Designed by Joseph Fiebiger*
*Photo: P.A. Fiebiger, Inc.*

*Page 37*
*Hand forged & repoussé skylight*
*Palm Beach Residence*
*Designed by Joseph Fiebiger*
*Photo: P.A. Fiebiger, Inc.*

*Page 38*
*Bow Bridge, Central Park*
*Photo: Fotolia: Autumn © John Anderson #10518673*

*Page 42*
*Cherry Hill Fountain, Central Park*
*Photo: P.A. Fiebiger, Inc.*

*Page 45*

*Caramoor, Katonah, New York*

*18th Century Swiss Gates after 1975 restoration*

*Photo: P.A. Fiebiger, Inc.*


*Page 47*

*Caramoor, Katonah, New York*

*Hand forgedf stair railing*

*Mott B. Schmidt, Architect*

*Photo: P.A. Fiebiger, Inc.*


*Page 50*

*Louis XVI stair railing for grand circular stair bronze cartouchés, bronze acanthus leaf ornaments and Baccarate chrystal with polished bronze handrail*

*Sneden's Landing, NY Residence*

*Designed by Rafa Varga and Joseph Fiebiger*

*Ca. 1968*

*Photo: P.A. Fiebiger, Inc.*


*Page 52*

*Hand forged & repoussé grilles for entrance doors*

*Sneden's Landing, NY residence*

*Designed by Joseph Fiebiger*

*Ca. 1968*

*Photo: P.A. Fiebiger, Inc.*

*Page 56*

*Harkness Theatre, New York City*

*Orchestra railing without decorative swags*

*Ca. 1974*

*Photo: Courtsey Harkness Foundation For Dance*

*Page 59*

*Gainesway Farm, Lexington, KY*

*Forged iron sliding gates*

*Photo: Courtsey Theodore Ceraldi*

*Page 64*

*The Old Senate Chamber*

*Photograph: Courtesy Architect of the Capitol*

*Page 65*

*Benches in the Rotunda*

*Photograph: Courtesy Architect of the Capitol*

*Page 68*

*Old Senate Chamber Franklin Stove*

*Photograph: Courtesy U.S. Senate Collection*

*Page 70*

*The Morgan Library, New York City*

*Entrance gates and side lites*

*Photo: P.A. Fiebiger, Inc*

*Page 74*

*The Morgan Library, New York City*

*Bronze entrance gates and side lites*

*Photo: P.A. Fiebiger, Inc*

*Page 74*

*The Morgan Library, New York City*

*Bronze entrance gates and side lites*

*Photo: P.A. Fiebiger, Inc*

*Page 77*

*The Morgan Library, New York City*

*Bronze entrance gates and side lites*

*Running Eros*

*Photo: P.A. Fiebiger, Inc*

*Page 82*

*The Frick Collection, New York City*

*Forged fences and piers*

*Photo: P.A. Fiebiger, Inc*

*Page 83*

*The Frick Collection, New York City*

*Entrance portal to the gardens*

*Photograph: Courtsey of © Peter B. Kaplan*

*Photo: P.A. Fiebiger, Inc*

*Page 101*

*Metropolitan Museum of Art, New York City*

*Sullivan Stair - Restored*

*American Wing - Metropolitan Museum of Art*

*Ca. 1983*

*Photo: P.A. Fiebiger, Inc*

*Page 208*

*Gennaro "Bruno" Ranieri stands proudly with the completed spires*

*Photo: P.A. Fiebiger, Inc.*

*Page 214*

*Signature plaque with names of all the artisans that made the decorative copper elements*

*Photo: P.A. Fiebiger, Inc.*

Back Cover

Bow Bridge, Central Park

Autumn © John Anderson #10518673

# Schedule of Major Commissions

Knickerbocker Club, New York City (1913). Balcony railings and electrical fixtures. Delano and Aldrich, Architects.

The White House, Washington, DC (1923). Repoussé medallions of the Presidential Seal as door stops.

Residence of Dr. Phillip Cole, Irvington, NY (1926). Entrance gates made with forging bronze, children's chariot, stair railings. Delano and Aldrich, Architects.

Residence of Hubert E. Rogers, Briarcliff Manor, NY (1928). Stair railings, bronze garden gates with the motif of Espalier trees, and bronze trellis porch. Delano and Aldrich, Architects.

Union Club, New York City (1933). Stair railings, balcony railings, electrical fixtures. Delano and Aldrich, Architects.

Marjorie Merriweather Post, Washington, DC (1958). Louis XVI stair railing, entrance gates. Alexander MacIlvaine, Architect

Twenty One Club, New York City (1931). Fences, marquee, doors and Jockeys.

The Brick Church, New York City (1958). Cross, railings.

St. James Church, New York City. Repoussé pineapples as roof ornaments (1920). Removal of pineapples (1950), Moore and Hutchins, Architects. Exterior stair railings (1959). Moore and Hutchins, Architects.

Music Building, 1939 World's Fair (1937). Decorative repoussé ornament for facade. Delano and Aldrich, Architects.

Pocantico Hills, Tarrytown, New York (1920-1958). Restoration of entrance gates, pedestrian gates, fences and grilles. Mott B. Schmidt, Architect.

Baseball Hall of Fame, Cooperstown, New York (1949-1957). Iron railings, gates and canopy, baseball motif. Moore & Hutchins, Architects.

Residence of Mr. and Mrs. Paul Mellon, Middleburgh, Virginia (1952-1968). H. Page Cross, Architect.

American Numismatic Society, New York City (1957). Decorative iron gates. Block & Hess, Architects.

Trinity Episcopal Church, Upperville, Virginia (1954-1965). Hand forged iron railings, gates, grilles, fanlights, chandeliers, lecterns, hardware. H. Page Cross, Architect.

Trinity Church, Wall Street, New York City (1963-1965). Fences, gates, and stair railings. Adams and Woodbridge, Architects.

Mr. and Mrs. Skitch Henderson, New York City (1965). Iron fence and gate.

Mr. and Mrs. Vincent Sardi, New York City (1966). Window grilles, lighting fixtures.

Pomery House, Cooperstown, New York (1966). Decorative, hand forged iron railings, hardware and electrical fixtures. Moore & Hutchins, Architects.

Residence of Mr. and Mrs. Paul Mellon, New York City (1964). Railings and fences. H. Page Cross, Architect.

Residence of Mr. & Mrs. Edward L. Stephenson, Wildcat Mountain, Warrenton, Virginia (1967). Hand forged stair railing, fire tools with and irons.

Residence of Mr. & Mrs. Joseph Mulford, The Plains, Virginia (1967). Stair railings. William B. Dew, Jr., Architect.

Iranian Embassy, New York City (1967). Louis XVI stair railing.

Residence of Mrs. Vincent (Brooke) Astor, New York City (1967). Directoire stair railing. H. Page Cross, Architect.

Residence of Mrs. Enid Haupt, New York City (1968). Stair railing, grilles and fanlights.

Residence of Mr. & Mrs. Russell Aitken, New York City (1968). Louis XVI stair railing. McMillen, Inc., Interior Designers.

Residence of Mrs. Rebekah Harkness, Sneden's Landing, New York (1967-1969). Louis XV, Louis XVI stair railings, balcony railings, grilles, doors, spiral stairs and hardware. Florence Clark and Rafa Varga, Interior Designers.

Residence of Mr. & Mrs. Deane Johnson, Los Angeles, California (1968-1969). Louis XVI stair railings  and electrical fixture brackets and hardware. McMillen, Inc., Interior Designers.

Residence of Mr. Del Coleman, New York City (1969-1970). Louis XVI gates, grilles and fanlights. Helen Franklin Morton, Interior Designer.

Residence of Mrs. Aye Simon, New York City (1970-1971). "Modern" stair and stair railing, plated with nickel and satin chrome.

St. Paul's Chapel, New York City (1971). Iron gates. Adams & Woodbridge, Architects.

Residence of Mrs. Vincent (Brooke) Astor, Briarcliff Manor, New York (1971- 1972). Driveway gates, hardware and restoration of bronze gates, repoussé fruit motif, H. Page Cross, Architect.

Residence of Mr. Robert Goelet, New York City (1970-1973). Five flights of curved stair railings, balconies, grilles, fences, gates, fanlights. H. Page Cross, Architect.

Residence of Mrs. Enid Haupt, Palm Beach, Florida (1971-1972). Modern stair railing, Louis XVI skylights and torcherés.

Riverside Church, New York City (1972). Structural steel cribbing for the restoration and re-tuning of the bells in the carillon.

Restoration of Bow Bridge, Central Park, New York City (1972-1974). Restoration and reconstruction of the Frederick Law Olmstead, Calvert Vaux cast iron pedestrian bridge. Platt, Wyckoff & Coles, Architects.

Harkness Theatre, New York City (1971-1974). Louis XVI stair railings, balcony railings and doors. Enrique Senis, Interior Designer.

Caramoor Center for Music and the Arts, Katonah, New York (1928-1940). Modification of Swiss gates and Spanish gates, new garden gates and stair railings.

Caramoor (1972). Stair railings and balcony railings. Mott B. Schmidt, Architect.

Caramoor (1972) Restoration of Art Deco doors and electrical fixtures.

Caramoor (1975-1976). Restoration of Swiss and Spanish gates (1975-1976).

Morgan Library, New York City (1974) Restoration of main entrance gates, restoration of iron fences.

Morgan Library (1976-1978). New bronze windows, decorative hand forged stair railings and hardware for new wing. Platt, Wyckoff & Coles, Architects.

United States Capitol, Washington, D.C. (1974-1976).
Decorative of iron columns in Old Senate Chamber. Architect of the Capitol.
Replication of Benjamin Franklin's Wood Burning Stoves, Old Senate Chamber. Architect of the Capitol and Poor and Swanke, Architects.
New fences for East Front of Capitol.
Restoration of fences for statues of War and Peace. Architect of the Capitol.
New bronze stair railings entrance to Senate Chamber. Architect of the Capitol.

The Frick Collection, New York City (1975-1977). Execution of hand forged and repoussé fences, piers and gates, duplicating those which exist around the property, all stylized versions of those at the Grand Trianon, Palace of Versailles. Harry van Dyke, John Barrington Bailey, Architects.

The Frick Art Reference Library, New York City (1976). Decorative bronze stair railings for exterior stair. Harry van Dyke, Architect.

Cathedral of St. John the Divine, New York City (1976). Restoration of the Baptistry gates and of St. Martin's Chapel.

Metropolitan Museum of Art, American Wing, New York City (1978-1980). Restoration and reconstruction of Louis Sullivan's copper plated, cast iron stair from the Chicago Stock Exchange.

The Pierpont Morgan Library, New York City (1979-1980). Design and execution of vitrines for "Michaelangelo and his World."

Gainesway Farm, Lexington, Kentucky (1979-1981). Execution of hand forged, Italian Renaissance, gates, grilles and hardware. Theodore Ceraldi, Architect.

Residence of Mr. Gilbert Kahn, Miami, Florida (1980). Decorative, hand forged stair railing.

Park Avenue Synagogue, New York City (1979-1981). Decorative iron entrance gates. Professor James Rush Jarrett, Architect.

Residence of Mr. Stinor Gimbel, New York City (1980-1982). Window grilles and doors.

Cherry Hill Fountain, Central Park, New York City (1979-1981). Cast bronze and repoussé fountain (finial). Gerald Allen, Architect.

Juddmont Farm, Berkshire, England (1980-1981). Hand forged bronze hardware. Theodore Ceraldi, Architect.

Metropolitan Museum of Art, Michael C. Rockefeller Wing (1981-1982). Mounts for art objects, installation of all major art objects.

Residence of Mr. J. Shephard, Williamsburg, Virginia (1981-1982). Polished bronze and polished steel curved stair railings.

Residence of Mr. & Mrs. Marshall Rose, New York City (1982). Glass and iron terrace railings.

Residence of Barbaralee Diamonstein Spielvogel, New York City (1983). French doors and Solarium.

Cartier, New York City (1982). Replication of existing bronze windows, allowing for new bullet resistant glass (1-3/16" thick).

Residence of Mrs. Mary B.D.T. Semans, New York City (1982-1983). Restoration of decorative copper mansard roof. Recipient of The New York Landmarks Conservancy Chairman's Award for Excellence. Gerald Allen, Architect.

Metropolitan Museum of Art, Frank Lloyd Wright Room (1982). Polished bronze railings.

Residence of Mr. & Mrs. John Alison, Washington, D.C. (1982). Polished bronze and steel, curved stair railing. Thomas A. Buckley, Interior Designer.

Metropolitan Museum of Art, Department of Painting Conservation (1982). Reconstruction of 19th century easels for the performance of painting restoration.

The Frick Collection, New York City (1982). Design and execution of decorative bronze stair railings, main entrance. Harry van Dyke, Architect.

City of Philadelphia, Tower of the City Hall (1982-1983). Performance of "pilot" project for future comprehensive restoration.

Metropolitan Museum of Art, American Wing (1983). Restoration of hand forged stair railing for stone pulpit. Structural mechanism to support Sounding Board and Angel.

Metropolitan Museum of Art, Vanderlin Panorama (1983). Iron railings with labels.

Ballantrae, Inc., New York City (1983-1984). Decorative stair railings and balcony railings.

Sutton Square Park, New York City (1983). Iron fences and gates.

Central Park Conservancy, The Carousel (1983). Decorative fences with "horse" motif.

St. Thomas Church, New York City (1983). Communion Railing and Sacristy fixtures. Gerald Allen, Architect.

The Lawrenceville School, Lawrenceville, New Jersey (1983). Oak and bronze vitrine.

Mission of the State of Kuwait to the United Nations (1983-1984). Modifications to stair railings.

Medallion Oil Company Houston, Texas (1983-1984). Decorative, cast bronze directory and mail box.

Residence of Mrs. Jean Nidetch, New York City (1983-1984). Polished stainless steel, modern, stair railings.

Residence of Mr. & Mrs. Joseph Hudson, Houston, Texas (1983-1984). Replication of decorative, hand forged and cast bronze door with operable glass lite and fanlight.

Restoration of Statue of Liberty, New York Harbor (1982-1986). As a joint venture participant with the Nab Construction Company.

Replication of original armature bars and saddles.

Disengagement of Torch and Flame,

Replication of "drum" or Torch with special fittings to attach the original Flame.

Fabrication of structural chassis' to enable proper transportation as an art object.

Remedial and restorative work at all damaged areas of copper skin.

Approximately 600 areas received attention. Most notable are the nose, eyes, lips, curls and upper body.

Ellis Island - Main Building, New York Harbor (1984-1987). As a joint venture participant with Simpson Metal Industries, (a division of the Nab Construction Corporation), Fred A. Munder, Inc. and L.H. Kent, Inc.

Decorative copper spires atop domes.

Decorative copper elements surrounding domes.

Decorative copper elements adorning clerestory.

Morgan Library, New York City (1985-1987). Restoration of bronze entrance gates.

Morgan Library (1987). Restoration of the statue "Eros", uncovered from the ruins of Pompeii.

Residence of Mrs. Mary B.D.T. Semans, New York City (1985-1987). Restoration of decorative iron and bronze marque, restoration of cast iron bay window, restoration of decorative, hand forged doors with over doors. Gerald Allen, Architect.

Residence of Mr. Bennett Lebow, New York City (1987-1988). Two Louis XVI stair railings with two matching sets of entrance doors.

Residence of Mr. Donald Trump, New York City (1986-1989). Stylized Louis XV stair, stair railings and gates.

Residence of Dr. and Mrs. John Sluder, Armonk, NY (1987—1988). Decorative iron railings and gates. Platt, Wyckoff and Coles, Architects.

The University of Pennsylvania, Furness Building, Philadelphia (1987-1988). Three decorative copper finials, replicating originals. Scott, Rauche and Brown, Architects.

Metropolitan Museum of Art, American Wing, New York City (1988-1989) Luce Collection. Modular easels inside vitrines, for display of art objects.

The Frick Collection, New York City (1988-1991) Restoration of decorative iron fences, gates and piers.

The J. Pierpont Morgan Library, New York City (1990-1991). New entrance gates and fence panels for handicap access. Iron doors, stainless steel planters, trellises and bronze railings for the new interior courtyard. Voorsanger and Associates, Architects.